3.98

KW-328-531

WITHDRAWN
FROM STOCK

Critical Guides to French Texts

Critical Guides to French Texts

EDITED BY ROGER LITTLE, WOLFGANG VAN EMDEN,
DAVID WILLIAMS

HUGO

Hernani *and* Ruy Blas

Keith Wren

Lecturer in European Studies,
University of Kent at Canterbury

Grant and Cutler Ltd
1982

27559

© Grant & Cutler Ltd
1982
ISBN 0 7293 0123 0

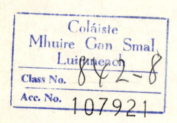

Coláiste
Mhuire Gan Smal
Luimneach
Class No. 842-8
Acc. No. 107921

I.S.B.N. 84-499-5685-4

DEPÓSITO LEGAL: V. 1.501 - 1982

Printed in Spain by

Artes Gráficas Soler, S. A. - La Olivereta, 28 - Valencia (18)

for

GRANT & CUTLER LTD
11 BUCKINGHAM STREET, LONDON W.C.2.

Contents

Acknowledgments

My grateful thanks are due to Professor Roger Little, advisory editor of the series, for his assistance and encouragement; to Dr Susan Taylor-Horrex, who read the manuscript and made many valuable comments and suggestions; to Mrs Janet Howarth, who uncomplainingly and efficiently typed the manuscript; and to my European Studies students, whose interest and enthusiasm constitute the source of this monograph.

Note on editions used

THERE is no good modern edition of either *Hernani* or *Ruy Blas* currently available from an English publisher. For both plays, therefore, I have used the helpfully annotated editions by Gérard Sablayrolles, published in the Nouveaux Classiques Larousse series (Paris, 1971), both accompanied by a useful set of contemporary 'Documentation Thématique'. I have used *line* numbers when referring to the text of the plays, *page* numbers when referring to that of the prefaces.

There exists in French an excellent scholarly edition of *Ruy Blas*, by Anne Ubersfeld (Annales littéraires de l'Université de Besançon, vols 121 and 131, Paris, Belles-Lettres, 1971-72), which comprises a historical and critical study of the play, a comprehensive scrutiny of the manuscript and variants, historical and contemporary documents, lexicon, and a very full bibliography. It is, however, a tool for the researcher rather than an edition for the general reader.

For the *Préface de Cromwell*, the most convenient edition is once again that published by Nouveaux Classiques Larousse in 1972 and edited by Michel Cambien.

When dealing with Hugo's other plays, I have used the uniformly excellent and exhaustively documented edition of the *Oeuvres Complètes*, edited by Jean Massin (Paris, Club du Livre, 18 vols, 1967-70). The collected edition of Hugo's *Théâtre*, by Raymond Pouilliart (Paris, Garnier-Flammarion, 2 vols, 1979) is in fact more convenient, with good critical introductions and critical apparatus, but unfortunately omits both *Cromwell* and *Les Burgraves*.

Italicised numbers in parentheses, followed by page references, refer to the numbered items in the bibliography at the end of this volume.

1

Introduction: the *Préface de Cromwell*

HUGO'S *drames* have tended to suffer at the hands of critics in the past because of the approach adopted. The plays have been seen primarily in a rather negative light, in terms of what they are not, or of what they react against, namely the persistence of the neo-Classical tradition of the seventeenth and eighteenth centuries, personified above all by Racine and Voltaire. To a very large extent, then, neo-Classical tragedy has been the critical yardstick by which Hugo's theatre has been judged. Whilst there is no doubt that this can be a valid approach, and one which Hugo himself invites in his own theoretical statements on drama, it is not the only one. It must not be forgotten that the first generation of Romantics, the *génération de 1820*, to which Hugo belonged, did not restrict their interests to purely literary matters. They also shared a concern for the social and political questions of the day, as may be seen in the poetry of Lamartine and Vigny, and the novels of George Sand. Hence, when we come to assess Hugo's theatre, we must try to understand its various component parts not only in the context of the battle between Romanticism and Classicism, but also as an exemplification of Hugo's ideas and theories about the society of his own time and that of the future. The object of this monograph is to suggest an interpretation of *Hernani* and *Ruy Blas* based on this twin axis, and to try and situate these two best-known (and best) of Hugo's plays in the context of his dramatic output as a whole (prior to 1843), indicating, as the analysis will show, how social and political concerns gain in prominence from one play to the other.

The grip of neo-Classical tragedy on the French theatre, dating from the mid-seventeenth century, had been paradoxically strengthened by the Revolution and especially by Napoleon, who disapproved of cultural innovation as a threat to the continuity he sought to establish with the legitimate monarchy of the past. In fact, eighteenth-century dramatists had already perceived the impending ossification of dramatic form and content: Voltaire made timid, but valuable, attempts to remedy this, whilst Diderot and Beaumarchais sought the abolition of tragedy in favour of the *genre dramatique sérieux*, though the plays which they produced to illustrate their theories were unfortunately not good enough to loosen the stranglehold of neo-Classicism. Their basic ideas, however – substitution of prose for verse, social relevance, didacticism, 'situations fortes' – were destined to recur, and it is generally accepted that the *genre dramatique sérieux* was the forerunner of the melodrama of the boulevard theatres.

Literary ferment began in earnest after the abdication of Napoleon. Most influential in this respect was Madame de Staël, who in her *De l'Allemagne* (1810), had provided detailed discussion of works of German literature, and made the younger generation eager to know more. She concentrated her attention on the German theatre, urging her compatriots to take it as a model and, more than anyone, endeavouring to stress that 'la tendance naturelle du siècle c'est la tragédie historique'.[1]

It proved easier to pontificate than to create. Translations of foreign authors flooded the market in Restoration France – Shakespeare, Walter Scott, Byron, Schiller and Milton were copiously sold and read – but the effect on the theatre was disappointing. Public taste had to be weaned away from neo-Classicism, and the great successes of the period were plays like Lebrun's *Marie Stuart* (1820), which sought to adapt foreign authors to pre-existing French norms. The reimposition of full censorship in 1820 made life no easier, and promoted the growth of a form of closet-drama, the *scène historique*, plays written to be read rather than performed, owing to their political tendentiousness. Manifestos abound-

---

[1] G. de Staël, *De l'Allemagne,* edited by Comtesse J. de Pange, Grands Ecrivains de la France, 5 vols (Paris, Hachette, 1958-60), II, 256.

ed – Stendhal's two pamphlets entitled *Racine et Shake-speare* (1823 and 1825) are the best-known – but theories were not successfully put into practice.

Hugo could not stand aloof from the debate, though his attitudes changed appreciably over the period. From a youthful zealot of the neo-Classics, who could write in 1820 that 'les pièces de Shakespeare et de Schiller ne diffèrent des pièces de Corneille et de Racine qu'en ce qu'elles sont plus défectueuses' (*5*, I, 604), he became an increasingly outspoken advocate of reform. His 1823 review of Scott's *Quentin Durward* sees drama as a reflection of all human life, in terms which point prophetically forward to the *Préface de Cromwell*: 'La vie n'est-elle pas un drame bizarre où se mêlent le bon et le mauvais, le beau et le laid, le haut et le bas, loi dont le pouvoir n'expire que hors de la création?' (*5*, II, 437).

The *Préface de Cromwell* itself, published in 1827, created an enormous stir: Théophile Gautier wrote that it 'rayonnait à nos yeux comme les tables de la loi sur le Sinaï' (*9*, p. 5). In fact it said little that was new, so much theorising had there been about the reform of the theatre, and owed its impact to its relative brevity, coupled with the sustained vigour of its style.

The *Préface de Cromwell* is Hugo's major theoretical document on the theatre, and has constantly been used by critics as a means of confronting his principles with his subsequent practice. We must therefore briefly consider its argument. It calls for the abolition of the unities of time and place, and the retention of the unity of action, 'la seule vraie et fondée' (*1*, p. 66). It rejects all imitation and all rules except those of nature – 'il n'y a ni règles, ni modèles' (*1*, p. 77) – arguing that 'tout ce qui est dans la nature est dans l'art' (*1*, p. 60), although a degree of selectivity must be exercised: art does not 'hold...the mirror up to nature', but uses a 'miroir de concentration' (*1*, p. 82), to give a sense of coherence. This is assisted by the retention of verse, 'la forme optique de la pensée' (*1*, p. 90), which preserves the *drame* from prosaism. Hugo's metre is the alexandrine, which he insists must be liberated in both form and content from the constraints of the *style noble* – 'un vers libre, franc, loyal, osant tout dire sans pruderie, tout exprimer sans recherche' (*1*, p. 90), which can be 'aussi beau que de la prose' (*1*, p. 91).[2]

Tragedy is to give way to the *drame*, 'la poésie complète' (*1*, p. 56), which is more suited to our Christian era, in that, like Christianity, it recognises the duality of man, the *sublime* and the *grotesque*. This is a complex point. It first of all implies the mixture of genres, 'car la poésie vraie, la poésie complète, est dans l'harmonie des contraires' (*1*, p. 60). It also operates in terms of characterisation. The representatives of the *grotesque* in the *drame*, who can be 'tour à tour bouffons et terribles, quelquefois terribles et bouffons tout ensemble' (*1*, p. 62), heighten the effect of the *sublime*. Sometimes the two elements can be mixed in one character, 'car les hommes de génie, si grands qu'ils soient, ont toujours en eux leur bête qui parodie leur intelligence' (*1*, p. 64). Sometimes the *grotesque* and the *sublime* dominate a character entirely, manifesting themselves 'par masses homogènes' (*1*, p. 64).[3]

The object of the exercise is, of course, more realism in character portrayal and in the representation of reality in general. The reality to be portrayed is a historical one. Hugo's concept of what constitutes historical reality is, however, rather unusual, and must be quoted at some length:

> L'art feuillette les siècles, feuillette la nature, interroge les chroniques, s'étudie à reproduire la réalité des faits, surtout celle des mœurs et des caractères, bien moins léguée au doute et à la contradiction que les faits, restaure ce que les annalistes ont tronqué, harmonise ce qu'ils ont dépouillé, devine leurs omissions et les répare, comble leurs lacunes par des imaginations qui aient la couleur du temps, groupe ce qu'ils ont laissé épars, rétablit le jeu des fils de la providence sous les marionnettes humaines... (*1*, pp. 82-83).

[2] A sarcastic aside directed at the many theorists who had urged the substitution of prose for verse. Stendhal, in *Racine et Shakespeare*, had memorably described the alexandrine as a 'cache-sottise'.

[3] Examples of entirely sublime characters are three Shakespearian heroines, Juliet, Desdemona and Ophelia (*1*, p. 50). Entirely grotesque characters include, on the 'bouffon' side, Juliet's nurse and Molière's George Dandin, and on the 'terrible' side, Richard III, Tartuffe and Mephistopheles (*1*, p. 65).

Hugo subsequently states that the prime aim of a historical drama is recreation of atmosphere, 'local colour', but warns that 'ce n'est point à la surface du drame que doit être la couleur locale, mais au fond, dans le cœur même de l'œuvre' (*1*, p. 84). I shall return to the question of Hugo's attitude to history when dealing with the plays.

Before we begin to compare Hugo's dramatic theory with his practice, a word must be said about his political views. The *Préface de Cromwell* contains a number of complimentary passing references to Napoleon, but Hugo's admiration for the Emperor was of comparatively recent date. The marital disharmony that subsisted between Léopold and Sophie Hugo had resulted in the young Victor being brought up by his mother and imbibing her Royalist politics. Her death in 1821, however, combined with Hugo's desire to marry, provoked a *rapprochement* with his father, a general in the Imperial army now retired on half-pay. This reunion, coupled with Hugo's increasing disenchantment with the restored Bourbon regime, induced a gradual shift towards Bonapartism in his political attitudes, a shift chronicled in his poetry of the 1820s, the *Odes*, and finally proclaimed in *Les Orientales* (1829), where he proclaims himself the Emperor's acolyte: 'Napoléon! Soleil dont je suis le Memnon!' (*5*, III, 601).

Although Hugo had embarked on his literary career as a poet, and continued to write a considerable amount of poetry throughout the major period of his dramatic production (1827-43), he clearly saw that the theatre offered him a much better chance of making his name. In 1826 he embarked on a play dealing with Oliver Cromwell, a rather unoriginal choice, since a number of other dramatists had also treated the subject recently, although none of these efforts had proved stageable. No more was Hugo's. Written in verse, it ran to an extraordinary 6,412 lines, and it seems clear that, by the time he had finished it, more than a year after beginning to write it, he could no longer really sympathise with the legitimism it expressed. It was published in December 1827, but, as we have seen, the preface, which was really an afterword (Hugo stresses that the ideas expressed in the *Préface de Cromwell* are 'des révélations de l'exécution' (*1*, p. 95) of the *drame* he has just written), created a greater impact than the play itself.

It seems clear that Hugo's approach to the problem of historical authenticity as exemplified in *Cromwell* was never going to produce a play of stageable length. I think it quite likely that Hugo himself realised this, in view of the remarks on the use of history contained in the *Préface de Cromwell*. He did not try to write another play until almost two years later, contenting himself in the interim with refurbishing *Amy Robsart*, a prose adaptation of Scott's *Kenilworth*, begun in 1822, and presenting it, albeit unsuccessfully, under the name of his brother-in-law Paul Foucher. In 1829, however, with two subjects in mind, he chose first to write *Marion de Lorme*. The reasons why *Hernani* turned out to be the play it was are closely connected with this decision, the results of which we must now consider more fully.

2

Hernani

25 février 1830! Cette date reste écrite dans le fond de
notre passé en caractères flamboyants: la date de la
première représentation d'*Hernani*! Cette soirée déci-
da de notre vie!... Bien du temps s'est écoulé depuis,
et notre éblouissement est toujours le même. Nous ne
rabattons rien de l'enthousiasme de notre jeunesse, et
toutes les fois que retentit le son magique du cor,
nous dressons l'oreille comme un vieux cheval de bataille, prêt à recommencer les anciens combats.
(*9*, p. 98)

GAUTIER'S enthusiasm aptly defines the barnstorming
effect of the first performance of *Hernani* on 25 February 1830,
a performance which, thanks largely to its attendant circumstances, has entered into the mythology of the theatre. It may,
I think, be reasonably doubted whether the 'bataille d'*Hernani*', as this occasion is habitually termed, was *per se* a significant phenomenon: it should rather be seen as the culminating
point in the persistent war of attrition between Romantics
and Classics in the theatre.

In view of the play's impact, it is perhaps ironical that
Hugo should have written it, as it were, on the rebound. It
was *Marion de Lorme*, composed between 2 June and 26
June 1829, which was intended to mark Hugo's triumphant
debut on the stage of the Théâtre Français. Eagerly accepted
by Baron Taylor, the Théâtre's director, the difficulties which
effectively prevented the play's performance were those rais-
ed by the censors, who objected to the depiction of Louis
XIII in Act IV, on the grounds that it reflected badly on
Charles X, his direct descendant. Hugo's subsequent negotiations, in the course of which he solicited, and obtained, an
interview with the King himself on 7 August 1829, are re-
counted in the eloquently entitled poem 'Le 7 août 1829', in

Les Rayons et les Ombres (1840) (5, VI, 33-37), which cun-
ningly implies the existence of a direct link between the interdiction of *Marion de Lorme* and the fall of the Bourbon
monarchy in 1830. A fuller and slightly less tendentious ac-
count is to be found in the autobiographical *Victor Hugo
raconté par un témoin de sa vie* (5, III, 1320-25).

Charles X refused to overturn the decision of the censors,
which had already been upheld by his minister, Vicomte de
Martignac. Instead, he offered Hugo financial compensation,
which the poet proudly rejected. The negotiations over *Marion de Lorme* having now reached an impasse, Hugo shelved
the play until it could be staged in more or less its original
form, and, towards the end of August, set to work on *Hernani*, which he completed within the space of four weeks. On 5
October 1829 it was accepted by the Théâtre Français, and
although there were further difficulties with the censors, they
were relatively unimportant and not viewed as matters of
principle by Hugo. Difficulties of a slightly different nature
with the actors, some of whom found Hugo's style too aud-
acious for their neo-Classical taste, were ironed out at re-
hearsal.

The two classic accounts of the 'bataille d'*Hernani*', both,
one suspects, a little romanced, are those of Hugo himself in
Victor Hugo raconté par un témoin de sa vie, and of Théophile Gautier in his *Histoire du Romantisme*, neither of
which I intend to summarise here. Although these two accounts are not always entirely in agreement with each other,
both make much of the pains to which the author went, and
indeed had to go, to secure a favourable reception for his
play, organising the occasion and marshalling his supporters
with the precision of a military operation to ensure that the
partisans of the Classics would be outvoiced. Such strategic
dispositions only underline the symbolic importance that
both sides saw in the performance. The famous Grandville
cartoon, showing the audience at each other's throats as Doña
Sol and Hernani lie dying on stage is perhaps not entirely ac-
curate, since the first-night audience had been won over by
the monologue of Don Carlos in Act IV, but pandemonium
returned at the second performance on 27 February, after the

almost uniformly hostile press given to the new play by first-night reviewers, and subsequent performances continued to be disrupted. However, if the performances were stormy, the receipts were excellent, and the play ran for the most unusually long period of 45 nights until the Doña Sol, Mademoiselle Mars, went on leave.

I think *Hernani* has perhaps been too often and too exclusively viewed as the triumph of Romanticism over Classicism in terms of dramatic form. Obviously the symptomatic significance of the 'bataille' is very considerable, but, without wishing to minimise this aspect, I feel we should try to see it in perspective. The play is, on one level at least, Hugo's answer to the Bourbon régime's decision to ban *Marion de Lorme*, a decision which, in Hugo's eyes, compromised the régime in its entirety, insofar as Charles X himself refused to cancel the interdiction. In this respect, *Hernani* is as much a political document as an aesthetic one, and I would argue that it represents Hugo's revenge on his opponents. His ambiguous preface, whilst apparently stressing the theme of artistic emancipation, by implication invites an interpretation with a political dimension, stating, for example, that the need for 'Tolérance et Liberté' (*2*, p. 31) applies to both politics and literature. And *Hernani*, despite its apparently inoffensive setting in sixteenth-century Spain, is very clearly a much more subversive play than its predecessor, the more so in that the portrait of Louis XIII which had provoked the censor's disapproval in *Marion de Lorme* is evidently borrowed from Alfred de Vigny's novel *Cinq-Mars* (1826), as opposed to constituting an overt political statement in its own right. I shall consider the nature and purpose of the subversiveness of *Hernani* when I come to deal with the political aspects of the play later in this chapter.

Let us first try to assess, however, the position of *Hernani* with regard to the *Préface de Cromwell*, its strictures on neo-Classical drama, and its prescriptions for its Romantic successor. It is possibly an error to assume that Hugo should have adhered strictly to the precepts of this manifesto, since there is no doubt that over the period under consideration (1827-43) his attitudes to drama did change, as we shall see.

Nevertheless, *Hernani*, written less than two years after the *Préface de Cromwell*, does hold especial interest as an opportunity for the embodiment of its precepts.

Hugo complies in *Hernani* with his own recommendation to abandon the two unities of time and place. The one is, to a certain extent, a function of the other, since the movement of the action from Saragossa (Acts I and II) to the château de Silva, somewhat imprecisely situated in the mountains of Aragon (Act III), then to Charlemagne's tomb at Aix-la-Chapelle (Aachen) (Act IV) and finally back to Saragossa (Act V) clearly requires more than a day to effect. The text is not explicit as to how long the action does take, but we do know that in Act I Don Carlos has just heard the news of the death of the Holy Roman Emperor Maximilian I, which actually took place on 12 January 1519. 'Mon aïeul l'empereur est mort. Je ne le sai / Que de ce soir' (282-83). Hence the action must begin after the news of Maximilian's death has had time to reach Don Carlos in Saragossa. The plot also encompasses the election of Don Carlos as Holy Roman Emperor, which historically took place on 28 June 1519, and Act V offers vague indications as to the new Emperor's current preoccupations, namely Luther and the Turkish sultan (lines 1838 and 1841), apart from which the season must be reasonably clement, since the nocturnal wedding feast is set on 'une terrasse du palais d'Aragon'.[1] We must, therefore, assume that the action concludes after Doña Sol, Hernani and Don Ruy Gomez have had time to return from Aix-la-Chapelle and before the onset of winter.

Where Hugo does depart from the *Préface de Cromwell* is with regard to the unity of action. This violation derives not from carelessness, despite the speed with which the play was written, but is caused by the political dimension of the play, and seems to be deliberate, since Hugo makes no attempt to minimise it. The duality of action is not apparent throughout

---

[1] The mention of the Turkish sultan 'Soliman' (Suleiman the Magnificent), would seem to suggest that Act V takes place in 1520, the date of his accession. However, he has already been anachronistically mentioned in line 1804, so no conclusion can be drawn.

the first three acts, which correspond neatly in theme to the original, but discarded, subtitle *Tres para una* (Three for one), their essential concern being the competition between the three male characters for the affections of Doña Sol. In Act IV, however, Hugo reduces the love-intrigue to minimal proportions (there is a passing reference to Doña Sol in lines 1386-88, then no further consideration of emotional matters until scene 4, when the Imperial pardon reunites Hernani and Doña Sol). Instead, he concentrates his attention on Don Carlos's meditations on the nature of Empire, as expressed in the celebrated, but dramatically superfluous, monologue of Act IV, scene 2. Having dominated Act IV, Don Carlos and his concerns then almost completely disappear from Act V, where the action reverts to the resolution of love-intrigue by way of the confrontation between Hernani and Don Ruy Gomez. In its simplest terms, if the play is essentially about Don Carlos's election as Emperor (we might note here the existence of another discarded sub-title, *La Jeunesse de Charles-Quint*), then Act V is superfluous, whereas if it is about the internecine rivalries between the characters for the love of Doña Sol, then Act IV is superfluous. If both acts are included, then the unity of action has been consciously violated, and has probably been violated for a good reason. This suspicion is increased by the rejection of both original subtitles in favour of the anodine third choice, *L'Honneur castillan.* I shall return to this point.

The mixture of genres advocated by the *Préface de Cromwell* is also not very convincingly achieved. The first scene of the play contains a certain amount of verbal comedy in the exchanges between Don Carlos and the duenna, Doña Josefa, culminating in the undignified concealment of Don Carlos in the cupboard, but there is little else, apart from the momentary humour of Don Carlos's exit from the cupboard (171), the cross-purpose discussion between himself and Don Ruy Gomez (303-36), and Don Ricardo's effortless acquisition of a string of titles (442, 1372, 1676), the last of which really pertains as much to social criticism as to comedy, as we shall see. It is not until *Ruy Blas* that Hugo really approaches success in integrating the mixture of genres in his drama.

No such criticisms can be levelled against him concerning the liberation of the alexandrine and the expansion of the poet's vocabulary. Hugo opens the play by nailing his colours to the mast: Doña Josefa's famous *enjambement*

> Serait-ce déjà lui? C'est bien à l'escalier
> Dérobé.   (1-2)

is followed almost immediately by three further examples of the same device, in lines spoken by Don Carlos:

> Suis-je chez Doña Sol, fiancée au vieux duc
> De Pastraña, son oncle, un bon seigneur, caduc,
> Vénérable et jaloux? dites? La belle adore
> Un cavalier sans barbe et sans moustache encore...   (5-8)

The stress patterns within the lines are also more varied: not only do we have the declamatory effect of such celebrated ternary alexandrines as:

> Je suis banni! Je suis proscrit! Je suis funeste!   (4+4+4)
>   (681)

but also a rather more subtle use of stress over longer sections of verse:

> Ciel! des douleurs étranges!...   (1+5)
> Ah! jette loin de toi ce philtre!... Ma raison   (1+8+3)
> S'égare. Arrête! Hélas! mon Don Juan, ce poison (2+2+2+3+3)
> Est vivant! ce poison dans le cœur fait éclore   (3+3+3+3)
> Un hydre à mille dents qui ronge et qui dévore! (2+4+2+4)
>   (2136-40)

I think we should note that these stylistic innovations are not gratuitous in their purpose or effect. Gautier's tongue-in-cheek comment on the first *enjambement* is apposite in this context:

> Ne voyez-vous pas que ce mot *dérobé*, rejeté et comme
> suspendu en dehors du vers, peint admirablement l'es-
> calier d'amour et de mystère qui enfonce sa spirale dans
> la muraille du manoir!   (*9*, p. 110)

And if we study more closely lines 2132 to 2136, where
enjambement is also a major feature, we shall see that Hugo
is seeking to convey by the unusual 'broken' or dislocated
structure of the lines the action of the poison on Doña Sol.
Form is here a powerful device to convey meaning.

Hugo himself is perhaps the best celebrant of his own
achievement in liberating and expanding the dramatist's vocabulary, in the poem 'Réponse à un acte d'accusation' collected in *Les Contemplations* (1856):

> Je mis un bonnet rouge au vieux dictionnaire.
> Plus de mot sénateur! plus de mot roturier!
> Je fis une tempête au fond de l'encrier...
> Et je dis: Pas de mot où l'idée au vol pur
> Ne puisse se poser, tout humide d'azur!
> Discours affreux! – Syllepse, hypallage, litote,
> Frémirent; je montai sur la borne Aristote,
> Et déclarai les mots égaux, libres, majeurs.   (*5*, IX, 75)

Curiously enough, the effect of the expansion of vocabulary is a good deal less egalitarian than Hugo implies. The
abolition of the *style noble* does, undeniably, confer in some
degree a sense of reality on the language of the play, a reality
very much lacking in the products of Hugo's neo-Classical
contemporaries. The example so well-known that Hugo himself includes it in 'Réponse à un acte d'accusation' is Don
Carlos's enquiry 'Quelle heure est-il?', which elicits the most
prosaic response 'Minuit bientôt' (463). We find, especially in
the speeches of Don Ruy Gomez, a good deal of reference to
the manners and customs of the time, and in this sense, the
expansion of vocabulary ties in with the requirement to recreate atmosphere, commonly known as local colour:

> Quoi! vous avez l'épée, et la bague, et la lance,
> La chasse, les festins, les meutes, les faucons,

> Les chansons à chanter le soir sous les balcons,
> Les plumes au chapeau, les casaques de soie,
> Les bals, les carrousels, la jeunesse, la joie.   (248-52)

The vestigial mixture of genres also provides opportunities for the democratisation of language that Hugo sought, as when Don Carlos, inspecting the cupboard which is to be his hiding-place, asks Doña Josefa:

> Serait-ce l'écurie où tu mets d'aventure
> Le manche de balai qui te sert de monture?   (23-24)

Paradoxically, however, this liberation permits an expansion of lyricism in certain parts of the play, most notably the love 'duets', which creates an operatic intensity far removed from the sense of reality I have mentioned. Chiefly memorable in lines such as

> Vous êtes mon lion superbe et généreux!   (1028)

so daring that Mademoiselle Mars replaced it in performance by

> Vous êtes mon seigneur vaillant et courageux

it permeates with sustained brilliance longer sections of verse, such as the following:

> Ah! qui n'oublierait tout à cette voix céleste?
> Ta parole est un chant où rien d'humain ne reste.
> Et, comme un voyageur, sur un fleuve emporté,
> Qui glisse sur les eaux par un beau soir d'été,
> Et voit fuir sous ses yeux mille plaines fleuries,
> Ma pensée entraînée erre en tes rêveries!   (1963-68)

These sections, despite their 'unreal' nature, effectively foster a charged and charmed atmosphere which remains one of the chief glories of the play. They are not in their effect, I think, susceptible of analysis: they contain a youthful ardour and idealism to which one must respond, if one responds at all, on a purely subjective and affective level. They compensate, however, for the areas of major weakness in the play as a whole, specifically the inadequacies of characterisation and the implausibility of the plot.

Whether we ascribe the failures of characterisation in *Hernani* to Hugo's endeavour to adhere to the *sublime/grotesque* antithesis postulated in the *Préface de Cromwell* as the basis of character creation, or whether we accept more generally that his gifts just did not really lie in that direction, the fact remains that none of the four main characters in the play is psychologically convincing. Hernani is persistently depicted in terms of a split personality, in whom there is little correlation between the suspicious and vengeful bandit and outlaw ('Hernani') and the tender and ardent aristocrat and lover ('Don Juan d'Aragon'). This is nowhere more evident than in Act V, when, after the sounding of the horn, Doña Sol addresses her newly-wedded husband by his correct name of Don Juan, and elicits the violent response

Nommez-moi Hernani! nommez-moi Hernani!
Avec ce nom fatal je n'en ai pas fini!   (1989-90)

Hernani represents the typical Romantic hero, at odds with society, himself and his love, or, in Hugo's impressive, if rather inflated, definition:

Une force qui va!
Agent aveugle et sourd de mystères funèbres!
Une âme de malheur faite avec des ténèbres!   (992-94)

With him, as with so many of his Romantic kin, is associated the idea of fate or destiny:

Où vais-je? je ne sais. Mais je me sens poussé
D'un souffle impétueux, d'un destin insensé.
Je descends, je descends, et jamais ne m'arrête.   (995-97)

Doña Sol is his redemption, a fact underlined by the constant use of terms associated with purity, innocence and paradise in describing her. But the use of this symbolism dissociates the two elements of Hernani's psychology, as Hernani himself states in the Act V duet:

> Je sais qu'il existait autrefois, dans un rêve,
> Un Hernani dont l'œil avait l'éclair du glaive,
> Un homme de la nuit et des monts, un proscrit
> Sur qui le mot *vengeance* était partout écrit,
> Un malheureux traînant après lui l'anathème!
> Mais je ne connais pas ce Hernani.   (1919-24)

We may, if we so choose, ascribe to 'Hernani' the facets of the *grotesque*, to 'Don Juan' those of the *sublime*, but there is no true resolution of the *sublime/grotesque* antithesis. The two sides of the character do not illuminate each other. They are mutually exclusive, and the character in consequence lacks all coherence.

As might be expected of a ministering angel, Doña Sol is entirely sublime. Totally devoted to Hernani (a point rather needlessly overemphasised by Hugo on her first appearance by her concern about her lover being soaked to the skin), she is wholly passive in her relationship with him, even in the face of his unreasonable, and quite unjustified, jealousy and suspicion (87, 893-915, 1701). Since she rarely appears except with Hernani, Hugo can do little more than present her as a paragon of perfect love. When on stage with other characters, however, she is rather more forthright, especially in her attitudes to Don Carlos, both in Act II, scene 2, and in her denunciation of him in Act III, scene 6: 'Roi don Carlos, vous êtes / Un mauvais roi' (1210-11). In her dealings with Don Ruy Gomez she is quietly determined, for we are left in no doubt that, if the marriage between them takes place, she will kill herself (725-6, 753, 789); and she shows signs of her old defiance in Act V, when, oblivious of honour's requirements, she seizes the phial of poison from Hernani in an endeavour to prevent the suicide that Don Ruy Gomez demands. Ultimately, however, these sporadic manifestations of spirit do not really convince us, simply because they are so sporadic.

Don Ruy Gomez is a little more successful. Hugo's depiction of the senile Spanish grandée is neither without humour nor pathos, and has its attractive touches: the old man maundering on about days of yore and offering needless and misplaced sympathy to Don Carlos for the death of his grandfather the Emperor (Act I, scene 3), the genuinely touching lament for the lost youth he mistakenly hopes to recapture by his marriage to Doña Sol (Act III, scene 1), and the outraged man of honour confronting his unworthy liege lord in the portrait scene (Act III, scene 6). The requirements of the plot, however, necessitate the transformation of Don Ruy Gomez in Act V into a demonic figure, the serpent who comes to destroy the happiness of the 'blest pair', Hernani and Doña Sol, in their new-found Eden, a point rather laboured by Hugo in a series of lexical references to death and Hell (1863-78). Once again, the introduction of symbolism dissolves the coherence of the characterisation: nothing remains of the *sublime* Don Ruy Gomez who resisted the King in Act III, unless we argue that his sense of honour, taken to the extreme, becomes cankered into *grotesque* and entirely negative.

The split-personality syndrome also, and most obviously, affects Don Carlos.[2] Here, the egotistical and dissolute character of the first three acts, who is willing to stop at nothing to gain his dubious ends (a case in point being his cynical manipulation of the situation at the château de Silva, whereby, failing to obtain the surrender of Hernani, he compensates himself by abducting Doña Sol), is miraculously and unexpectedly metamorphosed into a just and clement lord dispensing pardons to a confused band of conspirators, and placing the demands of the state above personal happiness. Once again, we have an example of antithetical characterisation: where Don Ruy Gomez moves from the *sublime* to the *grotesque*, and Hernani oscillates between the two, Don Carlos takes the reverse direction and moves from the *grotesque* to the *sublime*. In no one of these cases can Hugo be per-

---

[2] An interesting example of the contrast between the *political* and *psychological* demands of characterisation. As we shall see later, the character dichotomy in Don Carlos is absolutely central to the political meaning of the play.

ceived to have obeyed any clearly-defined psychological
logic.

If the characterization, at least from the angle of psychological consistency and sufficient motivation, is inadequate,
so too is much of the plot. No explanation is given of the
way in which Doña Sol and Hernani first met, nor do they
appear to know the first thing about each other: Doña Sol has
to explain to Hernani the reason for her intended marriage to
Don Ruy Gomez (87-88), whilst Hernani successively reveals
his present situation – 'Car, vous ne savez pas, moi, je suis un
bandit' (130) – and hints mysteriously at a former one – 'Vous
vouliez d'un brigand, voulez-vous d'un banni?' (170) – of
both of which Doña Sol is clearly oblivious. How Don Carlos
has encountered Doña Sol in order to fall in love with her is
similarly left unexplained. We are not entirely sure how Hernani was accepted by the conspirators in Act IV, since
although among their number there are 'quelques bandits, ga-
gés / Par Trève ou par la France' (1335-36), he is evidently
not one of these, and the remainder, as catalogued by Don
Ricardo in Act IV, scene 1, are members of the aristocracy,
who nowhere indicate that they know Hernani to be their
equal.[3] Moreover, since Don Ricardo has seen the conspirators (1339-40), we wonder why he has not arrested them,
and we are puzzled as to why the elector of Trèves (Trier)
should have chosen to lend them the tomb of Charlemagne in
which to conspire. How does Don Carlos know they are con-
spiring in Charlemagne's tomb? Why do the conspirators not
assassinate him when he appears at the sound of the first cannon shot at the end of Act IV, scene 3? It is all very implausible.

Given these inconsistencies in the plot, one might well expect a degree of weakness in the conduct of the action, and so
it proves. The devices of melodrama are everywhere in evidence, perhaps in part an inevitable consequence of the
rejection of the Classical interdiction of action on stage.

---

[3] A manuscript draft of Act II, scene 1 implied that Don Carlos's courtiers had some idea of Hernani's real identity, as did the conspirators, with
whom Hernani was already in collaboration. None of this remains in the
final version.

Much of Act IV is pure cloak-and-dagger stuff, with Gothic vaults, torches, passwords, oaths, the drawing of lots and the final *coup de théâtre* signalled by the firing of the cannon. Disguise is frequently resorted to: Don Carlos enters with his 'chapeau rabattu' to deceive Doña Josefa in Act I, Hernani appears as a monk in Act III, and Don Ruy Gomez is arrayed in a mask and a 'domino noir' in Act V. *Coups de théâtre* abound, examples being Don Carlos's exit from the cupboard in Act I, scene 2, the arrival of Don Ruy Gomez in Act I, scene 3, the arrival of Hernani in Act II, scene 2, Hernani's revelation of his identity in Act III, scene 3, and the sounding of the horn in Act V, scene 3 – 'j'en passe, et des meilleurs', to echo Don Ruy Gomez.

The great merit of *Hernani*, then, resides in a quality not normally perceived as dramatic, and for which the *Préface de Cromwell* makes no specific allowance, namely, lyricism. This, as I have suggested, is particularly in evidence in the love-duets between Hernani and Doña Sol, which punctuate the frenetic comings and goings of the rest of the play, and which I have termed 'operatic'. These duets provoke a deliberate heightening of tone, and a similarly deliberate reduction in the pace of the action, comparable only to that achieved by the monologue of Don Carlos in Act IV, scene 2. This reduction of pace is intentional because the play is – on one level, at any rate – about love. Hernani and Doña Sol are the perfect lovers – as exemplified in their selfless devotion to each other, and in their chastity – in a world where no place exists for their love, either socially (at least until Hernani reveals his true identity in Act IV), or, more specifically, in terms of the prevailing concerns of other characters. It as worth noticing that in no case does either Hernani or Doña Sol appear as a significant *initiator* of the action. Rather than impinging on the values of an alien world, they seek to escape, to render their love timeless, beyond worldly constraints, as Hernani stresses almost from the moment of his first entrance:

Cette heure! et voilà tout. Pour nous plus rien qu'une heure!
Après, qu'importe? Il faut qu'on oublie ou qu'on meure.

Ange! une heure avec vous! une heure, en vérité,
A qui voudrait la vie, et puis l'éternité!   (59-62)

Here we see, at one and the same time, the consciousness
of the ephemerality of existence and the desire to refute that
ephemerality. Whereas in *rational* terms Hernani is aware
that there must be an 'après', in *affective* terms anything subsequent to the 'heure' itself he rejects as irrelevant. This
attempt to eternalise the moment is inevitably foredoomed, at
least in life on earth: but we see also in these lines an indication of the only eternity which *can* be achieved, that of death,
hence a prophetic mirroring of the final union of the lovers in
the tomb. These conflicting elements, then, recur constantly
in the lyric duets which punctuate the play: rejection of contingent reality, endeavour to make the moment eternal, prefig-
uration of death. In Act II, scene 4, the lovers, absorbed in
each other, *become* oblivious of the fact that Don Carlos has
gone to raise the alarm, in that they *forget* their original consciousness of danger:

Eh bien, non! non, je reste.
Tu le veux, me voici. Viens, oh! viens dans mes bras!
Je reste, et resterai tant que tu le voudras.
Oublions-les! restons. Sieds-toi sur cette pierre...
Soyons heureux! buvons, car la coupe est remplie,
Car cette heure est à nous, et le reste est folie.
Parle-moi, ravis-moi.   (682-5, 689-91)

Since Hernani is in very pressing danger of being captured
by Don Carlos's troops, it is of course *literally* impossible for
him to fulfil the implications of a promise such as 'Je reste, et
resterai tant que tu le voudras'. The line nonetheless epitomises the search for an eternity in which their love can flourish,
the more so in that the subsequent line 'Car cette heure est à
nous, et le reste est folie' repeats the sense of lines 59 to 62,
quoted above.

The sound of the tocsin now adds the third element to our
equation, since in Hernani's mind it is assimilated to the
sound of wedding bells, rightly so in a sense, as, for the

lovers, wedding and death will ultimately follow one another so closely as to be indistinguishable from each other:

> DOÑA SOL
> Le tocsin!
> Entends-tu? le tocsin!

> HERNANI
> Eh non! c'est notre noce
> Qu'on sonne.   (696-98)

The end of the scene, with Doña Sol's vow 'Si tu meurs, je meurs!' (708) and the parting kiss, which is indeed, as Doña Sol predicts, 'le dernier' (710), foreshadows the *Liebestod* (love-death) of Act V, a duet in which the final and irremediable impingement of the real world on the timeless universe of the lovers can lead only to death. The aspirations of Doña Sol are ironically fulfilled:

> Regarde. Plus de feux, plus de bruit. Tout se tait.
> La lune tout à l'heure à l'horizon montait;
> Tandis que tu parlais, sa lumière qui tremble
> Et ta voix, toutes deux, m'allaient au cœur ensemble.
> Je me sentais joyeuse et calme, ô mon amant,
> Et j'aurais bien voulu mourir en ce moment!   (1957-62)

Doña Sol it is too, who, having drunk the poison, takes up Hernani's assimilation of wedding and death:

> Devions-nous pas dormir ensemble cette nuit?
> Qu'importe dans quel lit?...
> ... Voilà notre nuit de noce commencée!
> Je suis bien pâle, dis, pour une fiancée? (2134-5; 2147-8)

And she evokes their ultimate reunion in a Heaven which, one assumes, must recreate the ideal atmosphere of their moments of union and communion on earth:

> Vers des clartés nouvelles
> Nous allons tout à l'heure ensemble ouvrir nos ailes.
> Partons d'un vol égal vers un monde meilleur. (2151-53)

Thus far I have concentrated on the traditional and wide-ly-accepted view of *Hernani*, which argues that the play's technical and psychological weaknesses are largely redeemed by its lyricism and fervour. I should now like to turn my attention to the political implications of the play, which I think critics have generally underestimated, and try to show to what extent the play epitomises Hugo's political views as much as his aesthetic ones.

The political interpretation of *Hernani* hinges on the character of Don Carlos and his metamorphosis in Act IV. Don Carlos the King, as we see him in the first three acts, is both physically and morally unprepossessing. Hernani describes him as 'chétif et petit' (620), and Doña Sol produces a suitably crushing response when Don Carlos makes a scornful reference to the man she loves:

> Roi, je proclame
> Que, si l'homme naissait où le place son âme,
> Si Dieu faisait le rang à la hauteur du cœur,
> Certe, il serait le roi, prince, et vous le voleur![4]
> (493-96)

In the course of these first three acts, Don Carlos contrives to alienate, or to confirm the hostility of the three other major characters. Hernani's antagonism, as we learn in Act I, originally derives from a long-running family feud:

> Le roi! le roi! Mon père
> Est mort sur l'échafaud, condamné par le sien;
> Or, quoiqu'on ait vieilli depuis ce fait ancien,
> Pour l'ombre du feu roi, pour son fils, pour sa veuve,
> Pour tous les siens, ma haine est encor toute neuve! (88-92)

It is, however, further exacerbated by Don Carlos's strictly dishonourable intentions towards Doña Sol. Don Ruy Gomez

---

[4] This escaped the censor's pencil, although a similarly egalitarian declaration from Hernani did not. Hugo was obliged to substitute for the line 'Crois-tu donc que les rois à moi me sont sacrés?' (591) the less offensive 'Crois-tu donc que pour nous il soit des noms sacrés?'

renounces his loyalty to the King when Don Carlos abducts Doña Sol, whom Don Ruy Gomez is about to marry:

> Roi, pendant que tu sors joyeux de ma demeure,
> Ma vieille loyauté sort de mon cœur qui pleure. (1245-46)

And Doña Sol, the victim of the King's horse-trading, denounces as dishonourable the treatment meted out to Don Ruy Gomez by Don Carlos, in one of her most forthright utterances, which takes on its full significance in the light of the play's subtitle *L'Honneur castillan*: 'Altesse, tu n'as pas le cœur d'un Espagnol' (1212).

Since, moreover, Carlos has also contrived to alienate a number of other dignitaries who, as we learn in Act IV, are members of the conspiracy against him, it is arguable that, as a monarch, he is not a great success. His egotism is apparent both in his personal life, exemplified by his possessive attitude to Doña Sol, and in his political megalomania, illustrated by the series of intrigues he proposes in Act I to conduct with the Pope to ensure his election as Emperor. His courtiers, especially the grasping Don Ricardo, mirror in miniature his selfishness and *désinvolture*.[5]

Act IV, however, brings a transformation. The vicinity of Charlemagne's tomb assists Don Carlos to a clearer appreciation of the meaning of the Imperial dignity. It is no longer merely a case of amassing as much territory as he can, by fair means or by foul, as he seemed to believe in his discussion with Don Ruy Gomez (Act I, scenc 3). His progression to a higher and more responsible plane is signalled by his rejection of Don Ricardo's petty-minded squirrel mentality:

> Ah! tu me fais pitié,
> Ambitieux de rien! Engeance intéressée!
> Comme à travers la nôtre ils suivent leur pensée! (1372-74)

---

[5] Don Sancho seems to redeem himself in Act V by his discretion and the sincerity of his good wishes to Hernani and Doña Sol (1893-94), even though no previous hint has been given that he is any better than the other courtiers.

Don Carlos's 'pensée' still includes at this juncture the nec-
essity for trade in territories (1366-70) and for the merciless
disposal of rebels and conspirators (1344-49). The famous
monologue before the tomb of Charlemagne (1433-1600), however, signals the sudden elevation in his character, though
the commitment to capital punishment remains: 'Et dis-moi
qu'il vaut mieux punir que pardonner!' (1572). Not until after
the apocalyptic confrontation within the tomb is the transformation complete. The result, a general pardon, is singularly
reminiscent of the 'conversion' of Auguste in Corneille's
Cinna, which Hugo almost certainly took as his model, as
well as a reflection of widely-held Romantic attitudes to the
death penalty. The reaction to the clemency is electric, in
that Hernani, Don Ruy Gomez, and all the other conspirators, renounce their vengeance, and acclaim Don Carlos
as Emperor – 'Gloire à Carlos!' (1787).

Hugo is intent on stressing the point that Don Carlos is
now literally a new man. When Hernani, understandably as-
tonished by the pardon, and by the award of Doña Sol's hand,
asks 'Qui parle ainsi? le roi?', the immediate answer from
Don Carlos is 'Non, l'empereur' (1756-57), and the message
is driven home by Don Carlos's subsequent harangue to all
the conspirators:

Je ne sais plus vos noms, messieurs. Haine et fureur,
Je veux tout oublier. Allez, je vous pardonne!
C'est la leçon qu'au monde il convient que je donne.
Ce n'est pas vainement qu'à Charles premier, roi,
L'empereur Charles-Quint succède, et qu'une loi
Change, aux yeux de l'Europe, orpheline éplorée,
L'Altesse catholique en majesté sacrée.   (1780-86)

By the ex-conspirators' acclaim, the point is made: whereas Don Carlos the King had everyone against him, Charles-
Quint the Emperor has everyone on his side. A new social
order is created, based on the concept of 'tout oublier': significantly, the Emperor states 'Je ne sais plus vos noms'.
Everything is to start afresh. Symbolic of this universal reconciliation is the reintegration of the outsider Hernani by

means of the restitution of his titles. Having restored peace and tranquillity to the 'orpheline éplorée, Don Carlos now turns away from personal concerns to occupy himself unique-ly with matters of state:

> Eteins-toi, cœur jeune et plein de flamme!
> Laisse régner l'esprit, que longtemps tu troublas.
> Tes amours désormais, tes maîtresses, hélas!
> C'est l'Allemagne, c'est la Flandre, c'est l'Espagne.
> (1766-69)

The seeds of the contemporary political significance of this scene of universal reconciliation lie in the monologue of Act IV, scene 2, which we must now examine more closely, for it is here that Hugo makes his sustained attack on the Bourbon régime, and asserts his Bonapartism. It opens with an invocation to Charlemagne:

> Charlemagne, pardon! ces voûtes solitaires
> Ne devraient répéter que paroles austères.
> Tu t'indignes sans doute à ce bourdonnement
> Que nos ambitions font sur ton monument...
> Charlemagne est ici! Comment, sépulcre sombre,
> Peux-tu sans éclater contenir si grande ombre?
> Es-tu bien là, géant d'un monde créateur,
> Et t'y peux-tu coucher de toute ta hauteur?...
> Ah! c'est un beau spectacle à ravir la pensée
> Que l'Europe ainsi faite et comme il l'a laissée! (1433-42)

Within the context of the subject of the play, the apos-trophe is acceptable, in that Don Carlos aspires to become Holy Roman Emperor, a dignity first created for Charle-magne in A.D. 800. But already in the ode 'A la Colonne de la Place Vendôme' (1827) Hugo had linked the name of Charlemagne to that of Napoleon, and the full sense of the monologue can only be grasped if this parallel is borne in mind. From the angle of character psychology, of course, we have every right to criticise Don Carlos's subsequent dismis-sal of the importance of hereditary monarchy, when hitherto he has been so concerned to uphold its prerogatives. But Don

Carlos has now become Hugo's political mouthpiece, and the gospel he preaches derives not from the internal logic of the character, but from the words of Napoleon, recorded for posterity by Emmanuel de las Cases in the *Mémorial de Sainte-Hélène* (1822-23).

Like Napoleon in the *Mémorial*, Hugo/Carlos sees the Emperor as an incarnation of the popular and the divine will – *vox populi, vox dei – elected* monarch, superior in this respect to *hereditary* sovereigns:[6]

> Presque tous les états, duchés, fiefs militaires,
> Royaumes, marquisats, tous sont héréditaires;
> Mais le peuple a parfois son pape ou son césar.
> Tout marche, et le hasard corrige le hasard.
> De là vient l'équilibre, et toujours l'ordre éclate.
> Electeurs de drap d'or, cardinaux d'écarlate,
> Double sénat sacré dont la terre s'émeut,
> Ne sont là qu'en parade, et Dieu veut ce qu'il veut.
>
> (1445-52)

The apparent banality of the second hemistich of the last line in fact reiterates a point first made by Hugo in the *Préface de Cromwell,* where he had defined the poet's role as that of one who 'rétablit le jeu des fils de la providence sous les marionnettes humaines' (*1*, p. 83). Hugo in his manipulation of the character of Don Carlos thus gives us an *ex post facto* reinterpretation of history, where God stands in the same relation to humanity as does the dramatist to his characters.

The lines which follow, evoking the concept of the human and divine will – the 'idée' mentioned in line 1453 and again in line 1458 – epitomised in one man subjugating the power of hereditary monarchy, only serve to confirm the Bonapartism of the monologue. It is difficult not to see here an allu-

---

[6] References abound in Emmanuel de las Cases's *Mémorial de Sainte-Hélène* to Napoleon's elective status, e.g. 'Je n'ai point usurpé la couronne...je l'ai relevée dans le ruisseau; le peuple l'a mise sur ma tête: qu'on respecte ses actes'. The point is also made about the Imperial fresh start: 'Je suis monté sur le trône, vierge de tous les crimes de ma position...Est-il bien des chefs de dynastie qui puissent en dire autant?' (Paris, Garnier, 1961, I, 128).

sion to Napoleon's dominance in his heyday over the royal houses of Europe. We should not, on the other hand, accord serious attention to Hugo's division of hegemony between Pope and Emperor, a procedure which lends a degree of sixteenth-century historical colour to the monologue, but which has no relevance to Hugo's political creed, expressed now through nostalgia for bygone Napoleonic glories in the form of Don Carlos's ostensible lament for Charlemagne:

> Qu'il fut grand! De son temps, c'était encore plus beau.
> Le pape et l'empereur! ce n'était plus deux hommes.
> Pierre et César! en eux accouplant les deux Romes,
> Fécondant l'une et l'autre en un mystique hymen,
> Redonnant une forme, une âme au genre humain,
> Faisant refondre en bloc peuples et, pêle-mêle,
> Royaumes, pour en faire une Europe nouvelle... (1484-90)

Hugo's second theme, allied to the first, is the power of the people, deriving, as we have seen, from their implicit association with God. The people choose their Emperor (an argument dear to Napoleon's heart) but have their Kings imposed upon them, by virtue of which fact bad Kings must expect to be dethroned. Mankind is an ocean, keeping the pyramid of the social hierarchy afloat, menacing the fragile equilibrium of hereditary monarchy:

> Base de nations portant sur leurs épaules
> La pyramide énorme appuyée aux deux pôles,
> Flots vivants, qui toujours l'étreignant de leurs plis,
> La balancent, branlante, à leur vaste roulis,
> Font tout changer de place et, sur ses hautes zones,
> Comme des escabeaux font chanceler des trônes. (1529-34)

And Hugo includes an overt reference to the close association between the people and Napoleon, evoking the latter's tomb on sea-girt St Helena:

> Ah! le peuple! – océan! – onde sans cesse émue,
> Où l'on ne jette rien sans que tout ne remue!
> Vague qui broie un trône et qui berce un tombeau!
>   (1537-39)

With every reference to Charlemagne in the monologue susceptible of interpretation in a Napoleonic context, and given Don Carlos's conversion and general pardon (a clear parallel with the amnesties by which Napoleon endeavoured to reconcile the disaffected *émigrés*), we must perforce see the play in its true and subversive political colours. Its diatribes against hereditary monarchy imply hostility to the restored Bourbons, who are symbolised by the attitudes and the behaviour of Don Carlos prior to his conversion. Whereas *Marion de Lorme* had depicted Louis XIII only as a weak monarch, *Hernani* depicts Don Carlos as a bad one. The play's glorification of the Imperial dignity, coupled with Don Carlos's miraculous rebirth and the restitution of social order, unerringly point towards a vision of Hugo's ideal régime, still possible in 1830, for Napoleon's son, the Duc de Reichstadt, was yet alive, though a prisoner in Vienna.

The political dénouement of the play is completed in Act IV. The new Emperor disappears from the scene. God has worked out his purpose ('Dieu veut ce qu'il veut') by ensuring Don Carlos's election, even though the latter is only, as he learns, 'Empereur! – au refus de Frédéric le Sage!' (1698).[7] The fact that from a dramatic and psychological angle, the situation is most unsatisfactory is exemplified by Hernani's sudden submission – 'Oh! ma haine s'en va!' (1760) – which, after a feud of over thirty years' duration really will not do.[8] But Hugo's primary consideration is not verisimilitude. The act closes with Don Carlos supreme over a reconstructed social system, having discovered the secret of Imperial rule in clemency (1801-10), and now, having achieved the internal

[7] Historically the election of Charles V was unanimous. Hugo's misrepresentation of the facts seems designed once again to underline the existence of a divine purpose of which most men are unaware: the electors choose Frédéric, but God engineers his withdrawal. Dramatically, the situation is nonsensical, since if Frédéric considered himself unworthy, why did he not present himself for election in the first place?

[8] We learn in Act I that 'les pères ont lutté sans pitié, sans remords, / Trente ans' (97-98). Lines 93-94 indicate that the execution of Hernani's father took place while Hernani was still a child, and, as Hernani is now twenty (2032), the duration of the feud may well be nearer forty years than thirty.

pacification he never accomplished as King, ready to turn his attention to matters of international concern. The Napoleonic vision is thus triumphantly perpetuated.

It now becomes clear why Hugo cannot allow his shining political hero to become embroiled in the emotional tangles of Act V. The problem which remains to be solved is not central to the political significance of the play, although it does have political implications. It essentially involves the interrelationship of Hernani, Doña Sol and Don Ruy Gomez, a Gordian knot which cannot be severed by an Imperial *diktat*, the more so as Don Carlos now stands clear of matters of the heart (1766-69). The final *danse macabre* must take the floor without him.

In the ultimate love-duet between Hernani and Doña Sol, and the subsequent intervention of Don Ruy Gomez, we note a juxtaposition of celestial and demonic imagery. Doña Sol continues her redemptive role, the 'ange du Seigneur' (1930) welcoming Hernani to Paradise, where, like Adam, he begins life anew: 'Je n'ai rien vu, rien dit, rien fait. Je recommence, / J'efface tout, j'oublie' (1939-40). Don Ruy Gomez is 'un spectre échappé de la flamme, / Un mort damné, fantôme ou démon désormais' (2028-29), whom Don Garci, one of the revellers, has already compared with 'Lucifer / Qui vient nous voir danser en attendant l'enfer' (1877-78). In terms of Hugolian aesthetics we might see this as the supreme antithetical effect, the *grotesque* conferring its full relief on the *sublime*. But, without necessarily invalidating this interpretation, we can also see here an embryonic treatment of what will become the central theme of *Ruy Blas*, where each main character takes on a symbolic role as an incarnation of a specific social force, as well as a psychological and dramatic one. In this context Don Ruy Gomez appears as the embodiment of that past which he has so frequently invoked, and the sub-title *L'Honneur castillan* takes on a further, grimmer, meaning. Hernani's acceptance of the Imperial amnesty and his resumption of the name Don Juan d'Aragon indicate his willingness to accept the new political order, which ties in with the idea of beginning again (1939-40). But, by virtue of the values he has previously enshrined, embodied in his oath sworn to Don Ruy Gomez in Act III, he is still in fee to the past, and it is the past, in the form of Don Ruy Gomez, that claims him. The providential design represented by the new Emperor thus appears as a general one, without scope to deal with individual cases, and the forces of the old order remain tenacious, though ultimately destined to defeat, as shown by the symbolic suicide of Don Ruy Gomez with the words 'Je suis damné' (2166) on his lips. Don Carlos can forget the past (1781), but Hernani, in whose words the concept of *oubli* often recurs, cannot. [9]

Whether we accept either or both of these interpretations, the fact remains that *Hernani* has two dénouements. From the political angle, the outcome is positive, but from the personal angle, which we may choose to perceive as possessing political overtones, the outcome is negative, the curtain descending at the end of Act V on a stage strewn with three corpses. This inability or unwillingness to reconcile the two constituent elements of the play will be repeated, albeit less blatantly, in *Ruy Blas*.

How do we judge the success or failure of the play? On a superficial level it is exciting, carrying the uncritical reader or spectator along by its verve. The Act IV, scene 2 monologue was abridged by the author for performance, but even this cannot disguise its dramatic irrelevance, though it has an undeniable epic *souffle*, and, for the audiences of 1830, a political immediacy which it has lost for us. The ardour of the lyricism is engaging, however, and, for a play written so quickly, it has considerable empathy with the period depicted. Hugo knew and loved Spain, and he captures in his portrait of Don Ruy Gomez some of the rigour of the Spanish character, despite the fact that the notorious concern of the Spaniards with their honour was something of a *lieu commun*. Hugo's talent for local colour, however, really derives

[9] The recurrence of the theme of *oubli* underlines the incoherence of the character. 'Don Juan' (the lover) seeks to forget the world around him, and be united with Doña Sol, whereas 'Hernani' (the bandit) refuses to forget his revenge, until, ironically, it is too late and the oath has been sworn.

from the conduct of the action, the detail of the decor, and from the enormous number of Spanish place-names and family-names which intersperse the text. Some of the directions regarding costume, on the other hand, are very cursory: Doña Josefa is described in Act I as 'vieille, en noir, avec le corps de sa jupe cousu de jais, à la mode d'Isabelle la Catholique' (2, p. 35) which is not very illuminating: shortly after, Don Carlos is described as wearing 'un riche costume de velours et de soie, à la mode castillane de 1519' (2, p. 35) which is distinctly off-hand. Doña Sol, Hernani and Don Ruy Gomez fare little better. It is possible to ascribe this negligence to the speed with which Hugo researched and wrote the play, since *Ruy Blas* shows a distinct improvement in this respect.

Even more open to criticism must be Hugo's cavalier treatment of historical fact. Of the four major characters, only Don Carlos really existed. Hernani takes his name from the Spanish border town of Ernani through which Hugo had passed on his way to Spain as a boy in 1811, and the effective union of the crowns of Castile and Aragon in 1479 meant that only the King of Spain could be prince of Aragon, so the character must be imaginary. Moreover, the traits of the Romantic hero are somewhat out of keeping with the behavioural patterns of sixteenth-century Spain. Doña Sol's name is drawn from the *Romancero general*, which Hugo's brother Abel had translated in 1821: it is, like the names of many other Hugolian dramatic heroines, symbolic of celestial light, purity and innocence. Don Ruy Gomez, who makes speeches crammed with anachronisms, is a name most probably borrowed from Alfieri's tragedy *Filippo*, where there is a final scene very similar to that of *Hernani* in which the character appears. Hugo's knowledge of the play would not have been first-hand, but derived from Sismondi's encyclopedic and influential work *De la littérature du midi de l'Europe* (1813). As for the King, it is nowhere historically attested that the real Don Carlos was a dissolute young man, his election to the Imperial throne took place at Frankfurt, not at Aix-la-Chapelle, and there is no record of any conspiracy against him at that time. Hence the historical basis for the action is practically non-existent, hinging as it does on one single event, the election of Don Carlos.[10]

We should, however, beware of over-emphasising this point, since Hugo has, to a degree, pre-empted criticism. His vision of history, as enunciated in the *Préface de Cromwell*, is reminiscent of that of his master Chateaubriand, implying as it does a form of divine guiding purpose, in the interests of portraying which the poet may allow himself considerable liberties in the manipulation of his subject-matter. I think this paves the way for a political interpretation of *Hernani*: curiously, it can also exempt Hugo from strictures on his characterisation, since if God is the supreme puppeteer, then by definition human beings are mere puppets, and Hugo has thus not belied his ideological beliefs, despite the fact that his observations on the *sublime* and the *grotesque* lead us to expect a more rounded character portrayal. In both these respects Hugo reveals a close similarity to his contemporary Alfred de Vigny, whose 'Réflexions sur la vérité dans l'art', dating, like the *Préface de Cromwell*, from 1827, appeared in 1829 as the preface to his novel *Cinq-Mars*.

Hernani remains Hugo's most popular play. Seen objectively, it really ought not to be, since it is such a haphazard affair, but it is a play almost impossible to dislike, despite its catalogue of defects. None of Hugo's other plays seems to me to combine swashbuckling excitement so effectively with lyrical fervour, and the genuine dramatic tension which surfaces, for example, in the portrait scene and at the end of the play. In this context I find that ultimately deficiencies of plot and characterisation pale into insignificance. Gautier's assessment of the play strikes me as exactly right, precisely *because* it does not attempt to analyse the charm, but simply succumbs to it:

[10] This aspect of the play is covered in some detail by Georges Lote (*12*, pp. 107-22), who makes the further point that a number of the situations and incidents of the play are imitated directly from plays by the Spanish dramatists Alarcón and Lope de Vega: perhaps hardly to be expected from the author of the *Préface de Cromwell*? Hugo's prefatory claim that 'le *Romancero general* est la véritable clé' (*2*, p. 33) of *Hernani* clearly needs to be viewed with some caution.

Le mérite principal d'*Hernani*, c'est la jeunesse. On y respire d'un bout à l'autre une odeur de sève printanière et de nouveau feuillage d'un charme inexprimable; toutes les qualités et tous les défauts y sont jeunes: passion idéale, amour chaste et profond, dévouement héroïque, fidélité au point d'honneur, effervescence lyrique, agrandissement des proportions naturelles, exagération de la force; c'est un des plus beaux rêves dramatiques que puisse accomplir un grand poète de vingt-cinq ans.

(quoted in *2*, p. 216)

3

From *Hernani* to *Ruy Blas*

BETWEEN the production of *Hernani* on 25 February 1830 and that of *Ruy Blas* on 8 November 1838, Hugo completed four more *drames*, all of which were ostensibly based on historical subject matter, and all of which were staged. He was also successful in mounting the previously banned *Marion de Lorme*, thanks to the short-lived abolition of censorship which followed the accession of Louis-Philippe in 1830. The first of these new plays, *Le Roi s'amuse* (1832), set in sixteenth-century France, was, like its immediate predecessors, in verse, but was suspended by the minister responsible after its first performance on the not entirely convincing grounds that 'dans un grand nombre de scènes... les mœurs sont outragées' (quoted in *14*, p. 139, note 2). The three subsequent plays were all written in prose, a direct contravention of the precepts of the *Préface de Cromwell*: they were, respectively, *Lucrèce Borgia* (1832), *Marie Tudor* (1833), and *Angelo, tyran de Padoue* (1835), of which Hugo wisely removed the settings to the Italy and England of the sixteenth century, which at least lessened the likelihood of further trouble with the censors.

None of these plays now retains any great hold on the public's affection, and their importance lies perhaps less in their intrinsic merit than in the prefaces which Hugo composed to accompany their publication, and which contain an exposition of his ideas about the significance of the theatre and the responsibility of the writer. Certainly the last sentence of the preface (1831) to *Marion de Lorme* is revelatory in the latter context. Hugo writes 'Pourquoi maintenant ne viendrait-il pas un poète qui serait à Shakespeare ce que Napoléon est à Charlemagne?' (*5*, IV, 467), and this new Napoleon of letters proceeds, in subsequent prefaces, to define his ideas on the social function of the theatre:

> Le théâtre, on ne saurait trop le répéter, a de nos jours
> une importance immense, et qui tend à s'accroître sans
> cesse avec la civilisation même. Le théâtre est une tri-
> bune. Le théâtre est une chaire...L'auteur...sait que le
> drame, sans sortir des limites impartiales de l'art, a une
> mission nationale, une mission sociale, une mission hu-
> maine...Il ne faut pas que la multitude sorte du théâtre
> sans emporter avec elle quelque moralité austère et pro-
> fonde.   (5, IV, 655-56)

These references to the political ('tribune') and, indeed,
quasi-religious ('chaire') purpose of the theatre seem a far cry
from the more obviously aesthetic concerns of the *Préface de
Cromwell*, and it is, I think, arguable that Hugo's departure
from the use of verse, which he had so resolutely advocated in
1827, is directly attributable to his preoccupation with reaching a wider public: 'Au siècle où nous vivons, l'horizon de
l'art est bien élargi. Autrefois le poète disait: le public; au-
jourd'hui le poète dit: le peuple' (5, V, 269).

However, notwithstanding his scathing attack on the July
monarchy in the preface to *Le Roi s'amuse*, culminating in
the sarcastic inquiry 'Est-ce qu'il y a eu en effet quelque
chose qu'on a appelé la révolution de juillet?' (5, IV, 524),
Hugo's didacticism in all these *drames* is not (with the partial
exception of *Marie Tudor*) essentially political. Whereas a
major theme of *Hernani* is the implementation of the providential design in the replacement of the old order by the
new, the breaking of the iron grip of social fatality, the subsequent plays are devoted rather to an analysis of this social
fatality in its *moral* ramifications. It is social fatality which
has made Marion de Lorme into a prostitute: 'Pauvre enfant!
toute jeune, ils auront / Vendu ton innocence!... / Marie, ange
du ciel que la terre a flétrie' (5, III, 854-55). It is social fatality
which has made Triboulet, in *Le Roi s'amuse,* into a rancor-
ous and spiteful court fool. It is social fatality which has made
Lucrèce Borgia into a monster, 'empoisonneuse et adultère...
inceste à tous les degrés' (5, IV, 675). It is, moreover, the persistence of this social fatality which promotes, in each case,
the tragic outcome of the *drame*: because he discovers
Marion to be a prostitute, Didier rejects the opportunity she

procures for him to escape the scaffold; because of the way he has alienated them in his role as court fool, the courtiers kidnap Triboulet's daughter Blanche, and hand her over to be seduced by the King; because of the revenge she wreaks on his friends for past humiliation, Lucrèce Borgia ends her own life at the hand of her beloved son Gennaro.

The contrast between these plays and *Hernani* brings about a most intriguing interpretative situation. *Hernani* had demonstrated the victory of providence in the political sphere, a victory embodied in the transformation of Don Carlos, whilst simultaneously stressing the predominance of fatality in the personal sphere. In *Marion de Lorme*, *Le Roi s'amuse* and *Lucrèce Borgia*, political concerns are, to all intents and purposes, absent, and fatality would thus appear to have a clear field.[1] This is not, however, entirely the case. As Hugo wrote in 1834:

> Au théâtre surtout, il n'y a que deux choses auxquelles l'art puisse dignement aboutir. Dieu et le peuple. Dieu d'où tout vient, le peuple où tout va: Dieu qui est le principe, le peuple qui est la fin. Dieu manifesté au peuple, la providence expliquée à l'homme, voilà le fond un et simple de toute tragédie depuis *Oedipe roi* jusqu'à *Macbeth.* La providence est le centre des drames comme des choses. (5, V, 41)

Although 'le peuple' plays no significant active role in Hugo's theatre prior to *Marie Tudor*, the theme of providence is nonetheless very much in evidence from a moral standpoint in the three plays I have briefly discussed. If social fatality destroys Marion's chance of happiness with Didier, she is nevertheless *morally* redeemed and purified by his love, and it is in this context that the hand of providence is made manifest. The original manuscript of the play made this

---

[1] The absence of political intention might be deemed contestable in the context of *Marion de Lorme*, with its depiction of the vacillating Louis XIII in complete subordination to Richelieu, but the play is so deeply indebted in this respect to Vigny's *Cinq-Mars* that it would be rash to see it as a political statement in its own right.

abundantly clear. Lines 1611 to 1618 given to Marion in the stage version are a replacement for the following lines which Hugo felt himself 'obligé de sacrifier aux susceptibilités inqualifiables de la portion la moins respectable du public':

> Fût-ce pour te sauver, redevenir infâme,
> Je ne le puis! – Ton souffle a relevé mon âme,
> Mon Didier! près de toi rien de moi n'est resté,
> Et ton amour m'a fait une virginité.   (5, III, 860-61)

Similarly, although Triboulet is punished for his vicious mockery and slander by the loss of his daughter, Hugo stresses that he too must be seen as morally redeemed by love, though of a different sort:

> Prenez la difformité *physique* la plus hideuse, la plus re-
> poussante, la plus complète; placez-la là où elle ressort
> le mieux, à l'étage le plus infime, le plus souterrain et le
> plus méprisé de l'édifice social; éclairez de tous côtés,
> par le jour sinistre des contrastes, cette misérable créa-
> ture; et puis jetez-lui une âme, et mettez dans cette âme
> le sentiment le plus pur qui soit donné à l'homme, le
> sentiment paternel. Qu'arrivera-t-il? C'est que ce senti-
> ment sublime, chauffé selon certaines conditions, trans-
> formera sous vos yeux la créature dégradée; c'est que
> l'être petit deviendra grand; c'est que l'être difforme de-
> viendra beau.   (5, IV, 654)

The same applies to Lucrèce, in the sense that her mater-
nal love for Gennaro redeems her 'difformité morale'.

It is thus, I think, erroneous to see these *drames* as entirely pessimistic, for those characters who fall victim to the tragic events of the plays paradoxically rise superior to them by
virtue of their moral rehabilitation. A similar theme, though
less efficiently developed, is seen in Hugo's weakest play,
Angelo, tyran de Padoue (1835), where the actress Tisbe
sacrifices herself to permit the realisation of the pure love of
Catarina and Rodolfo.

Although political comment is not entirely absent from
these plays, it is essentially subordinate to the moral theme. It

is in this context especially ironic that *Le Roi s'amuse* should have been banned, at least in Hugo's view, for political reasons, although it should be said that the portrait of François I is certainly unflattering: moreover the play, as well as containing such provocative lines as 'Un puissant en gaîté ne peut songer qu'à nuire' (5, IV, 544), also repeats the strictures on the court nobility previously seen in *Hernani*, most notably in Triboulet's speech beginning 'Courtisans! courtisans! démons! race damnée!' and in the celebrated lines:

> Non! il n'appartient pas à ces grandes maisons
> D'avoir des cœurs si bas sous d'aussi fiers blasons!
> Non, vous n'en êtes pas! – Au milieu des huées,
> Vos mères aux laquais se sont prostituées!
>   (5, IV, 585; cf. ibid. 1209)

Ultimately, however, the only play of this period that can really be said to concern itself much with political themes is *Marie Tudor.* This play prefigures *Ruy Blas* in a number of respects and therefore deserves some attention. Like *Ruy Blas* (and, indeed, like *Hernani* before it) it signals the inadequacy of the hereditary principle: the Queen, obsessed by her Spanish-Italian favourite, the shoemaker's son Fabiano Fabiani, neglects the welfare of her realm: 'Pendant que la reine rit, le peuple pleure...Jamais rien de si dur n'a pesé sur l'Angleterre' (5, IV, 774). It prefigures the later play also in its introduction of 'l'homme du peuple', Gilbert the engraver. This is the first time in Hugo's theatre that such a character figures in the action *en tant que tel* and in a positive light.[2] A further similarity with *Ruy Blas* may be seen in the use the dramatist makes of the character of Simon Renard, the Imperial legate at Marie Tudor's court, and the *meneur du jeu* insofar as the political action of the play is concerned. It is, however, curious to note that the circumstances in which these ap-

---

[2] As *Marion de Lorme* tells us nothing about Didier's birth, we ought not to assume that he is a commoner. Nor is *Cromwell* a vindication of the eponymous proletarian hero: see my 'Comment peut-on être Cromwell?' (*FMLS*, XVI, 3, 256-69).

parent similarities operate are very different from what they will prove to be in *Ruy Blas*. The Marie Tudor-Fabiani axis is a prefigurative parody of the Marie de Neubourg-Ruy Blas relationship.[3] Fabiani, promoted to the ranks of the English aristocracy by the Queen, uses his position to negative, rather than positive, effect: 'C'est une chose affreuse et insupportable de penser qu'un favori napolitain peut tirer autant de billots qu'il en veut de dessous le lit de cette reine!' (5, IV, 775). Meanwhile, the real 'homme du peuple', Gilbert, far from taking any firm political initiative, as Ruy Blas will do, is entirely passive in the hands both of the Queen and of Simon Renard, who, in his manipulative role, resembles Don Salluste de Bazan. However, whereas Don Salluste is an entirely negative force Simon Renard (as befits the emissary of Charles V, the hero of *Hernani*) comes down on the side of the angels: 'J'ai sauvé la reine et l'Angleterre' (5, IV, 851).

The plot of this rather incoherent play essentially involves the mobilisation of the people in political terms, albeit passively, and thus clearly represents an advance on *Hernani*. Gilbert is not originally interested in the political manoeuvrings of the great: 'Que les loups se dévorent entre eux! Que nous importe, à nous, la reine et le favori de la reine...?' (5, IV, 780). However, Fabiani has seduced Gilbert's fiancée, Jane, and Simon Renard uses this fact to draw Gilbert into the plot against Fabiani, as the instrument of the favourite's destruction. In terms which point forward to Don Salluste's view of the people in *Ruy Blas*, the Queen, temporarily alienated from Fabiani, defincs Gilbert's role in the plot hatched by Simon Renard and herself:

> Vous voulez vous venger, et moi aussi. Pour cela, j'ai besoin de disposer de votre vie à ma fantaisie...J'ai besoin qu'il n'y ait plus pour vous ni faux ni vrai, ni bien ni mal, ni juste ni injuste, rien que ma vengeance et ma volonté.   (5, IV, 804)

---

[3] The parodistic effect is enhanced by the insistence that the relationship between Marie and Fabiani is primarily sexual, thus running counter to the slightly unreal air of purity that characterises true and worthwhile relationships in the plays of this period.

Unfortunately, Hugo endeavours to combine political themes with moral considerations. Perhaps understandably, in view of the preoccupations of his previous plays, he is interested in Gilbert's attitude to the 'fallen' Jane, his sublime endeavour to yield her up to her seducer (whom he believes she loves), and his forgiveness of her (like Didier's of Marion) in the last act *journée* of the play. His almost total apathy with regard to the political situation is rendered more incomprehensible since, in the last act the people of London rise in revolt against the Queen, and bring the monarchy to its senses. It is the Imperial legate who foments this rebellion, and who warns the scornful Queen: 'Cédez, madame, pendant qu'il en est temps encore. Vous pouvez encore dire la canaille, dans une heure vous seriez obligée de dire le peuple' (IV, 837).[4] The dichotomy which exists between the politically conscious *peuple* and the apolitical *homme du peuple*, in itself a perpetuation of the twin dénouement of *Hernani*, will be resolved in *Ruy Blas,* where Hugo is more, though not completely, successful in uniting personal and political elements in one character.

Anne Ubersfeld's view is that *Marie Tudor* is a 'drame de l'histoire' rather than a 'drame historique', and, whilst we might be rather hesitant about accepting the former definition, in view of the ambivalence relating to the role of the people and its representative, we shall have no difficulty in agreeing with her rejection of the latter definition, and indeed in extending it to all the plays of this period. *Marion de Lorme* is perhaps the most successful in terms of the recreation of historical atmosphere, though in this respect it owes much to Vigny's novel *Cinq-Mars* (1826). The plot of this play is,

---

[4] This apprehensive awareness of the power that the people can unleash has been seen already in Don Carlos's monologue in *Hernani*, and is also in evidence in much of Hugo's poetry at this time, e.g.

> O rois, veillez, veillez! tâchez d'avoir régné.
> Ne nous reprenez pas ce qu'on avait gagné,
> Ne faites point, des coups d'une bride rebelle,
> Cabrer la liberté qui vous porte avec elle;
> Soyez de votre temps, écoutez ce qu'on dit,
> Et tâchez d'être grands, car le peuple grandit.   (5, IV, 380)

however, totally apocryphal. In *Le Roi s'amuse* and the prose *drames* the historical ·element is attenuated almost out of existence. Admittedly François I's footloose and fancy-free antics are well attested in the memoirs of the period, but when, in *Lucrèce Borgia* and *Marie Tudor* Hugo begins to take immense liberties with major and well-documented historical figures, turning the former into a sublime mother and the latter into a nymphomaniac, then we are indeed on dangerous ground. The prose *drames* also bear witness to increasing carelessness and lack of sensitivity in the use of historical documentation, indigestible dollops of which are thrown in as elements of exposition, sometimes with near-farcical results.[5]

Characterisation in these plays also becomes increasingly weak. They were written at great speed – *Le Roi s'amuse* took Hugo eighteen days to complete, and *Lucrèce Borgia* only twelve days – which may partly explain this inadequacy. Traditional Romantic prototypes reappear: Didier is the fated hero à la Hernani: 'mon astre est mauvais. / J'ignore d'où je viens et j'ignore où je vais. / Mon ciel est noir' (*5*, III, 782). So is Rodolfo in *Angelo*: 'Nous tuons qui nous aime' (*5*, V, 283). The heroines are sublime, or have sublimity restored to them: Catarina in *Angelo* and Blanche fall under the former heading, Marion, Lucrèce, Jane and Tisbe under the latter. The old and honourable Marquis de Nangis in *Marion de Lorme* closely resembles the prelapsarian Don Ruy Gomez: the debauched François I is a mirror image of the pre-Imperial Don Carlos. The *sublime/grotesque* antithesis is very distinctly to the fore in *Le Roi s'amuse* and *Lucrèce Borgia,* as we have seen, for it lies at the heart of the conception of the central characters. We see it also in *Marion de Lorme*, but its importance is, I think, attenuated from *Marie Tudor* onwards. Admittedly Hugo's formula for the Queen in the preface, 'Grande comme reine. Vraie comme femme' (*5*, IV, 754), suggests a reworking of the idea, but the character fails to live

---

[5] The exposition to *Marie Tudor* is generally recognised to constitute the best – or worst – example of this syndrome: Anne Ubersfeld rightly calls it 'lourde, embarrassée, semée de personnages encombrants...de chassés-croisés inacceptables et de jeux étranges avec les objets' (*14*, I, 201).

up to the prescription, although the dramatist is perhaps more successful in implementing the latter element of the equation than the former.

Hugo's abandonment of verse constitutes a further negative element. His prose is distinctly leaden, and fails to conceal the increasing note of *emphase* that disfigures all these plays, and which, in turn, is exacerbated by the fact that Hugo tended to write with particular performers in mind.[6] The wilder excesses of Didier's or Marion's outpourings are rendered more acceptable when clothed in verse, but the hothouse style of a speech such as the following betrays all too clearly its links with the *drame bourgeois* and its degenerate offspring, the melodrama:

> Je me coucherai le jour à tes pieds, la nuit à ta porte ...Je serai pour toi quelque chose de moins qu'une sœur, quelque chose de plus qu'un chien. Et, si tu te maries, Gilbert...et si ta femme est bonne, et si elle veut bien je serai la servante de ta femme. Si elle ne veut pas de moi, je m'en irai, j'irai mourir où je pourrai.   (5, IV, 833)

The use of prose also seems to coincide with Hugo's increasingly crude application of melodramatic techniques. *Lucrèce Borgia* and *Angelo*, both set in Italy, have the necessary Renaissance apparatus of poisons and antidotes, secret passages, processions of monks chanting the *De profundis*, cataleptic trances, and – in *Angelo* – a splendid moment when Catarina, drawing back the curtains of her bed, discovers a block and axe positioned there in readiness for her decapitation. *Marie Tudor* has a first *journée* filled with cloak-and-dagger business involving a mysterious Jew from Brussels who ends up in the Thames, and a third *journée* centred around a torchlit procession to the gallows accompanied by rumblings of popular discontent.

---

[6] In particular, Marie Dorval. The 'ton Dorval' is especially in evidence in some of the 'pathétique' speeches of the female characters. See Descotes (7, p. 217) for an interesting analysis of Hugo's development of a speech in *Marion de Lorme* with this actress in mind.

Our dismissive view of these plays was not entirely shared by the audiences of the 1830s – *Lucrèce Borgia* was a very considerable success when first produced, although *Marie Tudor* and *Angelo* were not so fortunate. Interesting as they are, however, in a study of the development of Hugo's preoccupations as a dramatist over this turbulent period in French history, it is, nonetheless, something of a relief to turn from such literary mediocrities to a consideration of Hugo's acknowledged masterpiece, *Ruy Blas.*

4

Ruy Blas

Si l'auteur de ce livre a particulièrement insisté sur la
signification historique de *Ruy Blas*, c'est que, dans sa
pensée, par le sens historique...*Ruy Blas* se rattache à
Hernani. Le grand fait de la noblesse se montre, dans
Hernani comme dans *Ruy Blas*, à côté du grand fait
de la royauté...Entre *Hernani* et *Ruy Blas*, deux siècles de l'Espagne sont encadrés; deux grands siècles,
pendant lesquels il a été donné à la descendance de
Charles-Quint de dominer le monde; deux siècles que
la Providence, chose remarquable, n'a pas voulu
allonger d'une heure, car Charles-Quint naît en 1500,
et Charles II meurt en 1700...Dans *Hernani*, le soleil
de la maison d'Autriche se lève; dans *Ruy Blas*, il se
couche.   (*3*, p. 41)

THE emphatic way in which Hugo links his new play, *Ruy
Blas*, to its predecessor, *Hernani*, in the preface to the published edition of the former, is perhaps symptomatic of an
evolution in his attitude to the theatre. Rather unusually,
three years had elapsed since the production of *Angelo, tyran
de Padoue* (1835), disrupting the rhythm of a play a year
which Hugo had effectively maintained since *Cromwell*
(1827). Although a number of reasons of a non-literary nature can be adduced to explain this hiatus, it seems at least
arguable that Hugo was conscious of the extent to which his
concern to reach a wider audience through the medium of
prose had harmed his credibility as a serious dramatist, and
that his reversion, in *Ruy Blas*, to the form which had charac-
terised the success of *Hernani*, indicates a desire to reassert
his reputation.[1] In this context the resolute association of the

---

[1] Hugo's silence between 1835 and 1838 relates also to more practical
difficulties with regard to the Comédie Française. The details of the complicated transactions, culminating in the foundation of the Théâtre de la Renaissance, of which *Ruy Blas* was the inaugural production, may be found in A.
Ubersfeld (*14*, I, 282-312).

two plays in the last two paragraphs of the preface to *Ruy Blas* becomes that much more comprehensible.

So, for the first time since *Le Roi s'amuse* (1832), Hugo employs the verse form, again adopting that 'vers libre, franc, loyal, osant tout dire sans pruderie, tout exprimer sans recherche' (*1*, p. 90) adumbrated in the *Préface de Cromwell*. The requirement of writing in verse certainly did not impede the speed at which he habitually wrote (begun on 5 July 1838, the manuscript of the play was completed on 11 August, and the first performance given on 8 November), and in terms of dramatic naturalism I would argue that verse is an advantage, since the overblown prose Hugo had been writing in his previous *drames* was far from being natural. A further positive element in *Ruy Blas* is the dramatist's greater discretion in the use of melodramatic techniques, although we could hardly maintain that they are under-used: *Ruy Blas* has its fair share of coincidences and *coups de théâtre* (the Act IV entry of Don César is the best example of both). Moreover, the preface, whilst not denying the didactic content of the play, nonetheless elevates that didacticism to a more 'philosophical' level. It also implies that such considerations are rather less exclusively the province of *Ruy Blas* than they had been of its immediate predecessors, signalling the play's appeal on the level of human and dramatic interest as well. The depth of historical documentation, as evidenced in the *Note*, is a further indication of a renewed desire for respectability, the more so as the play demonstrates that Hugo has, in fact, absorbed his material to a much greater extent than he had in *Marie Tudor* (1833), despite its impressive source-list.

Another link between *Hernani* and *Ruy Blas*, and consequently a differentiation between these two plays and those of the intervening period, is that, from the didactic point of view, they concern themselves primarily with *political* rather than *moral* issues. The preface, indeed, is very insistent on the political dimension of *Ruy Blas*. The first, and by far the fullest, interpretation of the play that it offers, is set firmly under the heading of 'la philosophie de l'histoire' (*3*, p. 18), and we are told that 'le sujet philosophique de *Ruy Blas*, c'est le peuple aspirant aux régions élevées' (*3*, p. 21). The preface

thus orientates us firmly in the direction of political symbolism for (as in *Hernani*) what Hugo calls philosophy of history
is, by virtue of its almost complete rejection of historical par-
ticularism, essentially disguised contemporary political comment.[2]

We must therefore devote some attention to Hugo's analysis in the preface of the 'historical' situation of the play. He
offers a highly schematic vision of a society ostensibly pre-
sided over by a monarchy in decay, in this case that of the
Spanish Habsburgs under their last representative, Charles II.
The aristocracy, in this ruinous position, divides itself into
two categories:

> Comme la maladie de l'Etat est dans la tête, la noblesse,
> qui y touche, en est la première atteinte. Que devient-
> elle alors? Une partie des gentilshommes, la moins
> honnête et la moins généreuse, reste à la cour. Tout va
> être englouti, le temps presse, il faut se hâter, il faut
> s'enrichir, s'agrandir, et profiter des circonstances.   (*3*,
> p. 36)

This tendency is represented in the play by Don Salluste de
Bazan. The second category is represented by Don César de
Bazan, whom Hugo makes, symbolically, into Don Salluste's
cousin:

> L'état désespéré du royaume pousse l'autre moitié de la
> noblesse, la meilleure et la mieux née, dans une autre
> voie. Elle s'en va chez elle, elle rentre dans ses palais,

---

[2] It is significant that Hugo discusses what is apparently a specific historical situation in highly generalised terms. He writes of the 'moment où une
monarchie va s'écrouler' (*3*, p. 33), and his subsequent descriptions of Don
Salluste and Don César nowhere expressly relate to late seventeenth-century
Spain. It is only after having described them in detail that he particularises to
any degree whatever: 'Si le double tableau que nous venons de tracer s'offre
dans l'histoire de toutes les monarchies à un moment donné, il se présente
particulièrement en Espagne d'une façon frappante à la fin du XVIIe siècle'
(*3*, p. 37). The implication is that if such phenomena occur in all monarchi-
cal regimes 'à un moment donné', then they are occurring in the France of
1838. Hugo's characterisation of the people is, needless to say, similarly
unparticularised.

> dans ses châteaux, dans ses seigneuries. Elle a horreur
> des affaires, elle n'y peut rien...Il faut s'étourdir, fermer
> les yeux, vivre, boire, aimer, jouir.   (*3*, p. 36)

This mode of behaviour, however, leads, in the case of Don
César, to bankruptcy, since his sense of timing proves less
than perfect:

> Un beau matin, il lui arrive un malheur. C'est que,
> quoique la monarchie aille grand train, il s'est ruiné
> avant elle...Oublié et abandonné de tous, excepté de ses
> créanciers, le pauvre gentilhomme devient alors ce qu'il
> peut: un peu aventurier, un peu spadassin, un peu bo-
> hémien.   (*3*, pp. 36-37)

We shall see that the family relationship between Don Salluste and Don César, whilst admittedly necessary in terms of
the plot structure of *Ruy Blas*, is much more significant on
the level of political interpretation.

In the social stratum beneath the aristocracy

> on voit remuer dans l'ombre quelque chose de grand, de
> sombre et d'inconnu. C'est le peuple. Le peuple qui a
> l'avenir et qui n'a pas le présent; le peuple, orphelin,
> pauvre, intelligent et fort; placé très bas, et aspirant très
> haut; ayant sur le dos les marques de la servitude et
> dans le cœur les préméditations du génie...Le peuple,
> ce serait Ruy Blas.   (*3*, pp. 37-38)

It is here that the new play most clearly rejoins the political
preoccupations of *Hernani*, as expressed in the vision of the
people's role included in Don Carlos's monologue (Act IV,
scene 2). Hugo now introduces into his play a politically active member of the popular classes, achieving in this respect
an advance on *Hernani*, and on the unsatisfactory *Marie
Tudor*. Ruy Blas acts as both a physical and conceptual
embodiment of these political ideas.

Anne Ubersfeld, in her interpretation of this play, ob-
serves that 'c'est l'agonie d'une monarchie, et c'est l'agonie de
toute monarchie' (*5*, V, 657). In other words, we should not

be misled by Hugo's 'historical' division of society into two classes, aristocracy and people, for his description of Don Salluste's preoccupations mirrors his own hostile attitude to the Orleans monarchy. The final poem of *Les Voix Intérieures* (1837) had stigmatised the materialism and corruption rife in Louis-Philippe's bourgeois administration, 'ces trafiquants vils épris d'un sac d'argent' (5, V, 646), and threatened them with the poet's ire. *Ruy Blas* fulfils, more directly and effectively than any of the preceding *drames*, the precept of the preface to *Lucrèce Borgia*: 'mener de front désormais la lutte politique, tant que besoin sera, et l'œuvre littéraire' (5, IV, 653).

The weight accorded to the political interpretation of *Ruy Blas* clearly indicates that we are to consider as secondary the so-called human and dramatic interpretations: 'le sujet humain, c'est un homme qui aime une femme; le sujet dramatique, c'est un laquais qui aime une reine' (3, p. 40). This allegorical approach, whereby each of the three characters mentioned above becomes the symbol of a class or of one aspect of a class, works well on the whole. It does, however, have its drawbacks, principally with respect to the dénouement, which in political terms is confused, and to the role of the Queen.

The clarity of political definition afforded the other characters is not extended to the Queen, who seems to represent a rather nebulous ideal towards which the people aspires: 'le peuple, valet des grands seigneurs, et amoureux, dans sa misère et dans son abjection, de la seule figure qui, au milieu de cette société écroulée, représente pour lui, dans un divin rayonnement, l'autorité, la charité et la fécondité' (3, p. 38). This is much less precise a formulation than those employed for the other characters, and the next paragraph confirms the ambivalence of the Queen's role, which will beset the play: Hugo here fails to distinguish, as he manages to do for the other three characters, between the *political* as opposed to the *human* and *dramatic* levels:

Maintenant, au-dessus de ces trois hommes qui, ainsi considérés, feraient vivre et marcher, aux yeux du spec-

> tateur, trois faits, et, dans ces trois faits, toute la monar-
> chie espagnole au XVIIe siècle...il y a une pure et
> lumineuse créature, une femme, une reine. Malheur-
> euse comme femme, car elle est comme si elle n'avait pas
> de mari: malheureuse comme reine, car elle est comme
> si elle n'avait pas de roi; penchée vers ceux qui sont au-
> dessous d'elle par pitié royale et par instinct de femme
> aussi peut-être, et regardant en bas pendant que Ruy
> Blas, le peuple, regarde en haut.   (*3*, p. 38)

As will be seen, this is an unsatisfactory description of the
role on the level of political symbolism – the concept of 'une
pure et lumineuse créature' is less than enlightening! – and
Hugo falls back on interpretations on the human and dramatic levels – 'une femme, une reine' – which manifestly fail to
match the interpretation of Ruy Blas – 'le peuple' – employed
in this equation. This confusion, perpetuated throughout the
play, will ultimately weaken its interpretation on the political
level.

I shall now consider the four main characters in the play
in the light of Hugo's prefatory observations. Given the
emphasis placed on political considerations in the preface,
this aspect will inevitably predominate in the following analysis, without, however, excluding elements of the other two
interpretative levels, the human and the dramatic.

In his *Note*, Hugo specifies that 'Don Salluste, c'est Satan,
mais c'est Satan grand d'Espagne de première classe; c'est l'or-
gueil du démon sous la fierté du marquis' (*3*, p. 199). Demonic attributes recur persistently throughout the lexis used
by Hugo to describe the character, from the preface onwards:
'quelque chose de monstrueux se développe dans le courtisan
tombé, et l'homme se change en démon' (*3*, p. 36). In the play
itself, Don Salluste is constantly referred to as 'diable', 'démon', 'serpent', 'mauvais ange'.[3] The intention here is no different from that which I have argued is to be seen in Act V of

---

[3] A. Ubersfeld's edition of *Ruy Blas* contains a particularly useful *Lexi-
que* of words and names, to which readers are referred (*4*, II, 125-211). The
word 'diable', for example, is shown to recur twenty times, in various con-
texts.

Hernani, in which Don Ruy Gomez is described in similar terms (it is also significant that Don Salluste's final appearance directly parallels that of Don Ruy Gomez). Like Don Ruy Gomez, Don Salluste represents the diabolic forces of social fatality barring the road to the paradise of a utopian future. A fragment pertaining to the unfinished *Les Jumeaux* (1839) neatly defines Hugo's view of characters such as Don Salluste in the order of things:

> Caïn, Abel, vos races sont encore dans le monde
> les justes, les héros
> Esclaves et tyrans, victimes et bourreaux,
> Caïn
> Abel dit: Providence! et toi: fatalité!   (5, V, 879)

and a similar image is employed by Don César to describe his cousin:

> Toute intrigue de cour est une échelle double.
> D'un côté, bras liés, morne et le regard trouble,
> Monte le patient; de l'autre, le bourreau.
> – Or vous êtes bourreau – nécessairement.   (1973-76)

In political terms it is, of course, symbolic that Ruy Blas, the embodiment of the people, should serve as Don Salluste's lackey, for Don Salluste's egocentricity admits of no approach to life other than that of total self-indulgence: 'Ouvrez les yeux pour vous, fermez-les pour les autres. / Chacun pour soi' (1334-35). He will have no truck with any attempt to alter the prevailing class structure:

> Soyez de votre état. Je suis très bon, très doux,
> Mais que diable! un laquais, d'argile humble ou choisie,
> N'est qu'un vase où je veux verser ma fantaisie.
> De vous autres, mon cher, on fait tout ce qu'on veut.
>   (1420-23)

The idea of the national interest is totally alien to him except insofar as it coincides with his own:

Les intérêts publics? Songez d'abord aux vôtres.
Le salut de l'Espagne est un mot creux que d'autres
Feront sonner, mon cher, tout aussi bien que vous...
Vertu? foi? probité? c'est du clinquant déteint.
                                        (1369-71, 1375)

He thus remains deaf to the appeal of Ruy Blas, who begs
him to consider that the fate of Spain hangs in the balance –
'Le salut de l'Espagne est dans nos probités' (1348). His
imperviousness to finer feeling, his ruthlessness and his re-
morselessness lead his former lackey to compare his machinations to the blind inevitability of the movement of a
juggernaut:

O mon Dieu! voilà donc les choses qui se font!
Bâtir une machine effroyable dans l'ombre,
L'armer hideusement de rouages sans nombre,
Puis, sous la meule, afin de voir comment elle est,
Jeter une livrée, une chose, un valet...   (1448-52)

If, indeed, in respect of his plans he speaks of 'objets sérieux'
(1384), and asks Ruy Blas 'Savez-vous qu'il s'agit du destin
d'un empire?' (1417), his concept of what this implies is totally different: he is plotting the destruction of the Queen to
satisfy his own personal animosity, albeit at the expense of
the public weal. In terms of the political symbolism of the
play, the hostility between Don Salluste and the Queen takes
on cosmic significance: in their opposition, the forces of
social fatality confront the forces presiding over the ideal
of social progression. This would explain the reasoning behind
one of Hugo's discarded titles for the play, *La Vengeance de
Don Salluste.*[4]

Don Salluste's plans to disgrace and destroy the Queen are
described in lexical terms which can be seen to represent an
extension of the demonic imagery used to characterise him.
This denizen of the infernal regions aims to entrap the Queen
by devious and subterranean devices – the words 'mine' and

---

[4] Hugo's other proposed title, *La Reine s'ennuie*, can be seen more in
terms of an implied pun on the title of his own *drame* of 1832, *Le Roi
s'amuse.*

'sape' are used, and the words 'piège' and 'trappe' occur eleven times in the description of his intentions. It is significant, too, that in the implementation of his plan, he lures the Queen to a small, closed room, which contains, symbolically, 'une seule fenêtre à gauche, placée très haut et garnie de barreaux et d'un auvent inférieur comme les croisées des prisons' (*3*, p. 105) – this is, indeed, the 'cachot' (1607) in which his prey is snared. Despite the apparent failure of his plans, and his death at the hands of Ruy Blas, the outcome of these machinations is, as we shall see, rather more ambiguous than the events would seem to suggest.

Don César de Bazan is the most important and significant comic character in Hugo's theatre since Saverny in *Marion de Lorme*. He also represents Hugo's most concerted attempt since *Marion de Lorme* to implement the precepts of the *Préface de Cromwell* with regard to the use of the comic in the *drame*. Act IV, which he dominates, and which bears his name, has been much admired, although I tend to find it rather tiresome, a victim of Hugo's persistent inability to know when to stop. Nonetheless, Don César must be counted as a major participant in the action of the play, and his virtual monopoly of Act IV is certainly not merely tangential to the main lines of the plot, nor to the play's meaning. In terms of characterisation he, like Don Salluste, does not evolve. He is presented as a seventeenth-century 'drop-out', a quixotic figure. Admittedly he accepts the use of criminal means such as highway robbery to keep body and soul together, yet, like a Spanish Robin Hood, he confines his depredations to those who can afford to incur them. Moreover, as a manifestation of one vestige of his previous social status, he refuses to participate physically in these escapades:

> J'ai toujours dédaigné de battre un argousin.
> J'étais là. Rien de plus. Pendant les estocades,
> Je marchais en faisant des vers sous les arcades.
> On s'est fort assommé.   (84-87)

His gentility is similarly in evidence in his reaction to Don Salluste's proposal to involve him in his projected revenge on the Queen – 'Je vis avec les loups, non avec les serpents' (260). On the surface, then, he appears to retain the best elements of both his conditions – the honour of the gentleman, and the companionship and fellow-feeling of his bohemian years, as witnessed by the affection he displays for Ruy Blas in Act I, scene 3. And yet this engaging ruffian, 'Cet homme, cet hidalgo, mendiant spadassin qu'un mot blesse', who 'Drape avec un haillon cinq cents ans de noblesse', is a profoundly ambivalent character in both dramatic and political terms (see *4*, II, 21). For all his attractive *joie de vivre* and his impulsive generosity, his contribution to the play's outcome is, as we shall see, essentially negative.

If we turn now to Ruy Blas, we are confronted with a character who, in realistic terms, seems singularly implausible. As W. D. Howarth remarks, 'socially and historically, the character seems thoroughly absurd, and we find it difficult to take seriously, particularly in a seventeenth-century Spanish setting, the notion of a lackey who becomes prime minister and who loves, and is loved by, a queen' (*11*, p. 184). To a certain extent, however, this observation may miss the point, for, as I have suggested when discussing the preface, it is clear that Hugo does not intend to portray history in any specific sense. Ruy Blas, as his name implies, is a composite of abstract qualities. His plebeian origin is indicated by the name Blas, probably borrowed from the adventurer-hero of Lesage's eighteenth-century picaresque novel *Gil Blas*. His genius and spiritual nobility are, however, indicated by his specifically aristocratic forename Ruy (a shortened form of Rodrigo). To be honest, Hugo's attempt to explain the presence of this cultivated soul in the guise of a lackey is not very convincing:

> Orphelin, par pitié nourri dans un collège
> De science et d'orgueil, de moi, triste faveur!
> Au lieu d'un ouvrier on a fait un rêveur.   (298-300)

Forced by hunger to take on the menial employment of a lackey in Don Salluste's household, he has caught sight of the Queen – 'Je l'attends tous les jours au passage' (383) – and fallen hopelessly in love with her. His infatuation leads him to walk a league every day to gather a bunch of forget-me-nots, her favourite flower – 'Elle aime une fleur bleue / D'Allemagne' (397-8) – and to clamber over the palace wall in order to leave them on a bench in her garden. (How he has discovered the Queen's enthusiasm for this flower is not made clear.) It is an injury suffered as a result of this activity which occasions the Queen's recognition of the identity of her mysterious admirer (Act II, scene 3).

The meeting with the Queen has a galvanic effect on Ruy Blas. Hitherto he has been weak, passive, dominated by his master Don Salluste – a domination symbolically illustrated by the livery he wears, and by his unquestioning obedience, culminating in his meek agreement to sell his soul, as it were, to his mephistophelean master:

> Ecrivez: –'Moi, Ruy Blas,
> 'Laquais de monseigneur le marquis de Finlas,
> 'En toute occasion, ou secrète ou publique,
> 'M'engage à le servir comme un bon domestique.'
> –Signez de votre nom.   (503-07)

Indeed, this passive acceptance of Don Salluste's will persists throughout the play until his final insurgence against it in Act V. Its continuation is illustrated by the fact that, when Don Salluste returns in Act III, his first instruction to Ruy Blas can be seen to follow on from the opening words of the play – 'Ruy Blas, fermez la porte, – ouvrez cette fenêtre' (1):

> L'air me semble un peu froid.
> Faites-moi le plaisir de fermer la croisée.   (1344-45)

And Ruy Blas himself recognises the hypnotic influence of Don Salluste: 'Dans ma vie et dans moi... / Il est maître' (1520-21).

This ineffectuality may well seem strangely at odds with the vigour with which Ruy Blas, under the guise of Don César de Bazan, duc d'Olmedo, pursues his policy of reforming the corrupt administration of the country, as exemplified in the famous tirade of Act III, scene 2. This character discrepancy can best be explained in terms of political symbolism, as we shall see, but it once again exemplifies the considerable difficulty Hugo experienced in making his characters credible in human terms as well as symbolically convincing.

It is not possible to discuss the galvanic effect of the Queen on Ruy Blas without remarking on the reciprocal effect of Ruy Blas on the Queen. Prior to his advent, the Queen is also a weak and ineffectual character, hedged about by court ceremonial in the oppressively forbidding figure of the *camerera mayor*, the Duchesse d'Albuquerque, who blocks her most modest initiatives. To the Queen's expressed wish to go out of the palace, she replies:

> Il faut, pour que la reine sorte,
> Que chaque porte soit ouverte, – c'est réglé! –
> Par un des grands d'Espagne ayant droit à la clé.
> Or nul d'eux peut être au palais à cette heure. (646-49)[5]

This physical imprisonment is symbolic of the moral and spiritual situation in which the Queen finds herself. It is of course no accident that the icon in her apartment represents Santa Maria Esclava. The presence of Ruy Blas liberates her in both respects. Somewhat improbably, the *camerera mayor* disappears, and the Queen takes charge of her own destiny, and of that of her people, first disposing of Don Guritan, whose jealousy threatens the life of Ruy Blas, then ensuring the latter's rapid promotion to the post of first minister:

> C'est moi, depuis six mois, tu t'en doutes peut-être,
> Qui t'ai fait, par degrés, monter jusqu'au sommet.
> Où Dieu t'aurait dû mettre, une femme te met. (1246-48)

---

[5] There is, unfortunately, a degree of inconsistency in Hugo's characterisation here. Although he spares no effort to impress upon us the claustrophobic and oppressive effect of her life at court, we have already learned in Act I that the dismissal of Don Salluste has been provoked by her (9-14). Power to achieve the removal of a minister hardly seems consonant with the ineffectuality depicted in Act II, scene 1. The same situation prevails in reverse in Act III, where the Queen, notwithstanding her instrumentality in the promotion of Ruy Blas, still speaks of the constricting effect of court ceremonial on her every desire (1258-63).

It is, therefore, the mutual love of the Queen and Ruy Blas
that transforms both of them into paragons of energy. The di-
mensions of love as a dynamic are underlined in Ruy Blas's
definition of his motives for acting against the ministers:

> Parce que je vous aime!
> Parce que je sens bien, moi qu'ils haïssent tous,
> Que ce qu'ils font crouler s'écroulera sur vous!
> Parce que rien n'effraie une ardeur si profonde,
> Et que pour vous sauver je sauverais le monde! (1210-14)

It is only the Queen's physical presence in Act V that can
move Ruy Blas to action against the scheming and manipulative Don Salluste.

The somewhat unlikely effect of true love on Ruy Blas
and the Queen is, despite the implication of the previous
quotation, primarily dictated by political concerns. Hugo
stresses throughout the play that the Queen has strong links
with the people – the alms she gives so freely to the beggars
(622), her delight in the song of the *lavandières* (719-34), and
her foundation of a hospice for the poor (2228) underline this
fact. So too does her description of her own childhood:

> Que ne suis-je encor, moi qui crains tous ces grands,
> Dans ma bonne Allemagne, avec mes bons parents!
> Comme, ma sœur et moi, nous courions dans les herbes,
> Et puis des paysans passaient, traînant des gerbes;
> Nour leur parlions. C'était charmant.   (699-703)

Her childhood experience of a 'classless' society has given
way to the grim reality of her position as Queen of Spain, in
which she is, paradoxically, a prisoner. Before Ruy Blas's
arrival, she manifests no interest in affairs of state (674-79),
and expresses her complete lack of any sense of direction
when she refers to herself as a 'Pauvre esprit sans flambeau
dans un chemin obscur!' (755).

Her imprisonment at the head of a rigid social hierarchy is
as real as that of Ruy Blas in his lackey's livery at its foot:
here too the carefree innocence and idealism of youth have
given way before the pressures of life in society:

Oh! quand j'avais vingt ans, crédule à mon génie,
Je me perdais, marchant pieds nus dans les chemins,
En méditations sur le sort des humains;
J'avais bâti des plans sur tout, – une montagne
De projets; – je plaignais le malheur de l'Espagne;
Je croyais, pauvre esprit, qu'au monde je manquais... –
Ami, le résultat, tu le vois: – un laquais!   (314-20)

The forces of social fatality, therefore, hold both Ruy Blas
and the Queen in their vice-like grip. Separated from each
other, these soul-mates are marooned on their respective
echelons of the social scale. Their meeting, a 'secours du ciel'
(808) in a rather different sense from that first understood by
the Queen, and their subsequent interaction, is instrumental
in commencing the breakdown of these barriers, as evidenced
by the famous tirade of Act III, scene 2, and by the Queen's
plea to Ruy Blas:

Duc, il faut, – dans ce but le ciel t'envoie ici, –
Sauver l'état qui tremble, et retirer du gouffre
Le peuple qui travaille, et m'aimer, moi qui souffre.
                                                    (1264-66)

It is here that we must pause, in order to try and evaluate,
in default of assistance from the author, the role of the
Queen. What, precisely, *does* she represent? Not royalty as
such: the inadequacy of the hereditary principle, already ex-
posed in *Hernani*, is exemplified in her husband, Charles II,
who, symbolically, never appears in the play – 'Charles II
d'Espagne n'est pas une figure, c'est une ombre' (*3*, p. 38).
The Queen now takes over his functions:

            Au fait, le roi, malade et fou dans l'âme,
Vit avec le tombeau de sa première femme.
Il abdique, enfermé dans son Escurial,
Et la reine fait tout!   (985-88)

The persistence of celestial imagery in the descriptions of her
both by Hugo in the preface and by Ruy Blas in the play indicates that she embodies some divinely-sanctioned providen-

tial force which acts as a magnet to the oppressed classes. I
think it is important, in this respect, to notice the ordering of
priorities in lines 1265-66 (quoted above) – the salvation of
the state and the people is given precedence over human
love. However, the development of this providential force is
clearly threatened by both the passive and the active forces of
social fatality, respectively the *camerera mayor*, symbolising
the inert and stultifying effect of outmoded social conven-
tions, and Don Salluste, symbolising the actively anti-progres-
sive nature of a specific social class (or classes). The preface,
we recall, defines the Queen's role as follows: she is the magnet for

> le peuple, valet des grands seigneurs, et amoureux, dans
> sa misère et dans son abjection, de la seule figure qui,
> au milieu de cette société écroulée, représente pour lui,
> dans un divin rayonnement, l'autorité, la charité et la
> fécondité.   (*3*, p. 38)

I think that the use of the key words 'divin rayonnement'
must lead us to perceive her in terms of the new society Hugo
envisages as rising, phoenix-like, from the ashes of the old. In
this context, the political and human levels of the play come
together in Act III, for Ruy Blas's assault on the councillors,
mini-Sallustes to a man, embodies his vision of a juster society, in which one class will no longer oppress the others, and
constitutes the political counterpart of his adoration of the
Queen: the angelism inherent in his description of her in
scene 4 is valid both in terms of human love and political
aspiration:

> Devant mes yeux c'est le ciel que je voi!
> De ma vie, ô mon Dieu! cette heure est la première.
> Devant moi tout un monde, un monde de lumière,
> Comme ces paradis qu'en songe nous voyons,
> S'entr'ouvre en m'inondant de vie et de rayons! (1276-80)

As if in confirmation of this view, Hugo specifies that the
Queen enters, in scene 3, 'avec la couronne en tête' from
the secret cabinet where she has been eavesdropping on the

Council. The effect of her new-found interest in affairs of state is in marked contrast to the situation obtaining when her husband used this 'réduit obscur' (1191):

> Là j'ai vu bien souvent Charles deux, morne et sombre,
> Assister aux conseils où l'on pillait son bien,
> Où l'on pillait l'état.   (1194-6)

The powerlessness of Charles II to prevent his venal ministers from demolishing the fabric of the state has now been replaced by the firm and energetic rule of Ruy Blas, inspired by the Queen. Her presence in the 'réduit' is symbolic of the new order. The bankruptcy of hereditary monarchy has yielded to a providential force governing through the people. This explains the Queen's equation of Ruy Blas at one and the same time with a King and with God – *vox populi, vox Dei*:

> D'où vient que votre voix
> Parlait comme devrait parler celle des rois?
> Pourquoi donc étiez-vous, comme eût été Dieu même,
> Si terrible et si grand?   (1207-10)

Retrospectively, therefore, we see in political as well as human terms the vindication of Ruy Blas's earlier self-definition as 'Ce misérable fou qui porte avec effroi / Sous l'habit d'un valet les passions d'un roi!' (439-40).

The return of Don Salluste thus neatly posits the terms of the dénouement. The focus of attention is on Ruy Blas, whose division between the constraints imposed upon him by the social fatality of the old regime and his aspirations towards the providential 'brave new world' of the future is skilfully symbolised by the disposition of scenes in this act: the interview with the Queen (scene 3) is followed by a monologue (scene 4), and the return of Don Salluste (scene 5), causing Ruy Blas to exclaim: 'J'étais tourné vers l'ange et le démon venait' (1312).

True to form, Ruy Blas does not move directly against Don Salluste, and his use of indirect measures is doomed to failure because of an intervention from an unexpected source. Instead of obeying Don Salluste's instructions to await him in

the small house he inhabits, he sends word of the Queen's
danger to Don Guritan, then leaves:

> Ne l'attendons pas. Cela le paralyse
> Tout un grand jour. Allons prier dans quelque église.
> Sortons. J'ai besoin d'aide, et Dieu m'inspirera! (1561-3)

God's signals at this juncture are not of the clearest. Ruy
Blas's calculations are thrown into jeopardy by the return of
Don César, who, paradoxically, proves instrumental in the
implementation of Don Salluste's plans. The words with
which he greets his cousin when they finally meet again, are,
in fact, quite the reverse of the truth:

> Depuis toute la matinée,
> Je patauge à travers vos toiles d'araignée.
> Aucun de vos projets ne doit être debout.
> Je m'y vautre au hasard. Je vous démolis tout. (1933-6)

He has already negated the precaution taken by the Queen,
who has sent the duenna, Dame Oliva, to ensure that the
message purporting to come from Ruy Blas is to be relied
upon. By killing Don Guritan, he similarly destroys any
chance of Ruy Blas's real, warning, message reaching the
Queen.

The role of Don César in the play is thus clearly ambiguous. In a sense, this has been evident from the beginning.
In Act I, under the name of Zafari, he is greeted by Ruy Blas
as a brother:

> Tous deux nés dans le peuple, – hélas! c'était l'aurore! –
> Nous nous ressemblions au point qu'on nous prenait
> Pour frères.   (286-8)

But they are brothers neither by birth nor, more significantly,
by class – a fact which Don César never reveals to Ruy Blas.
Nor does he experience any real understanding of or empathy
with Ruy Blas's torment, a point evidenced by his largely
meaningless interjections during Ruy Blas's despairing ac-
count of his passion for the Queen ('Là, ne te fâche pas'

(437)). The best he can do is to offer Ruy Blas liberation from his position in Don Salluste's household, by making over to him half the money Don Salluste has given him. Ruy Blas refuses: 'Non. C'est le cœur qu'il faudrait délivrer. / Non, mon sort est ici. Je dois y demeurer.' (463-4). There is no substance to this fraternity, because there is no substance to Don César. He lives on the margin of the world in which this conflict is fought, for he no longer belongs to it:

> Moi, qui n'ai pas souffert, n'aimant personne,
> Moi, pauvre grelot vide où manque ce qui sonne,
> Gueux, qui vais mendiant l'amour je ne sais où,
> A qui de temps en temps le destin jette un sou,
> Moi, cœur éteint, dont l'âme, hélas! s'est retirée,
> Du spectacle d'hier affiche déchirée...   (441-6)

His anachronistic situation is again stressed in Act IV:

> Je ne suis plus vivant, je n'ai plus rien d'humain,
> Je suis un être absurde, un mort qui se réveille,
> Un bœuf, un hidalgo de la Castille-Vieille.   (1860-2)

It is therefore highly significant that, in this situation of which he understands nothing ('J'habite dans la lune' (1841); 'J'arrive des pays les plus extravagants' (1864)), and despite his loathing of his cousin, all his actions are unconsciously geared to the furtherance of Don Salluste's designs. In other words, Don César ultimately reverts to type. The relationship in which he stands to Don Salluste proves to be symbolic of class solidarity amongst the aristocracy. Don Salluste's objectives are much nearer realisation at the end of Act IV than they were at the beginning – thanks to Don César.[6]

---

[6] It is noteworthy that a fraternal or quasi-fraternal relationship, nowhere previously apparent in Hugo's theatre (with the partial exception of the bond between Maffio and Gennaro in *Lucrèce Borgia*) should play such a predominant role, not only in *Ruy Blas*, but in *Les Jumeaux* and *Les Burgraves*. Moreover, the ambiguous or hostile nature of the relationship is apparent in all three plays. It has been suggested that this represents an exteriorisation of repressed feelings on Hugo's part about his brother Eugène, who died, insane, on 20 February 1837. The cause of his insanity, which declared itself on the

For Act V, therefore, Hugo has completed the political line-up of the play. Don Salluste has benefited from the unwitting assistance of Don César, and has dispensed with him before any of his more positive attributes can get in the way of the successful realisation of the plot. The title of the act – 'Le Tigre et le Lion' – is symbolic. The tiger is Don Salluste, the reference being to a speech by Don César in Act IV:

> Ah! mon très cher cousin, vous voulez que j'émigre
> Dans cette Afrique où l'homme est la souris du tigre!
> $\qquad$ (1597-8)

The constant references to the idea of the trap throughout the play have made it evident that, in this context, it is with Ruy Blas and the Queen that Don Salluste aims to play cat and mouse. The lion is Ruy Blas himself, and the reference here, to the tirade of Act III, scene 3, stresses that, in the final confrontation, he embodies the aspirations of his class:

> Ce grand peuple espagnol aux membres énervés,
> Qui s'est couché dans l'ombre et sur qui vous vivez,
> Expire dans cet antre où son sort se termine,
> Triste comme un lion mangé par la vermine!   (1135-8)

It is here that the dramatist unfortunately clouds the issue. As we have seen, Hugo argues that the play functions on both the level of political symbolism and of human and dramatic interest. But his failure clearly to explain the Queen's role in anything other than a human and dramatic context leads to a singularly unsatisfactory and confusing ending.

Don Salluste's success in entrapping the Queen with Ruy Blas constitutes, on the face of the matter, a victory for the forces of social regression over those of social advance. Effectively, however, his overweening sense of triumph proves his

day of Hugo's wedding to Adèle Foucher, had been Eugène's own secret love for his brother's fiancée. Significantly, Hugo's moving valedictory poem 'A Eugène Vicomte H.', in *Les Voix Intérieures*, evoked only idyllic childhood memories; it may be that later unhappiness, censored by the conscious mind, is progressively exorcised in terms of these fraternal relationships in the plays.

undoing, and the trap into which he has lured the Queen, the 'Maison mystérieuse et propre aux tragédies. / Portes closes, volets barrés, un vrai cachot' (1606-7), becomes his own death cell. Ruy Blas takes on the traits of the archangel Michael in a clear reference to the expulsion of Satan from Heaven:

> On écrase un serpent qu'on rencontre.
> –Personne n'entrera, ni tes gens, ni l'enfer!
> Je te tiens écumant sous mon talon de fer! (2174-76)

This providential imagery is doubled by the twin assimilation of Ruy Blas to Christ in the final scene of the play. First comes a re-enactment of the legend of St Veronica:

> Auprès de l'hôpital que vous avez fondé,
> J'ai senti vaguement, à travers mon délire,
> Une femme du peuple essuyer sans rien dire
> Les gouttes de sueur qui tombaient de mon front.
>
> (2228-31)

This is followed by a reference to the crucifixion itself:

> Permettez, ô mon Dieu, justice souveraine,
> Que ce pauvre laquais bénisse cette reine,
> Car elle a consolé mon cœur crucifié,
> Vivant, par son amour, mourant, par sa pitié!   (2245-48)

This is where the confusion sets in. Is Ruy Blas the providential figure, the archangel casting out the demon, or is he 'un laquais qui aime une reine'? He cannot be both. In terms of the co-ordination of characterisation and symbolism, Hugo falls at the last hurdle. The death of Ruy Blas, albeit formulated in terms of Christ-symbolism, seems a distinctly curious mode of exemplifying the victory of the forces of progress over those of reaction: it effectively leaves the Queen all dressed up with nowhere to go. It seems unsatisfactory, to say the least, that Hugo, having accorded so much importance to the political interpretation of the play, should conclude it in terms of a human and dramatic interest that takes precedence over politics, because there is no way in which the two can be made to fit each other.

Ultimately, therefore, what we find in *Ruy Blas* is another example of the twin-axis ending. Just as proved to be the case in *Hernani*, the implications of the dénouement are politically positive, but personally negative. Don Salluste is destroyed, the Queen recognises Ruy Blas as a man of the people, calling him by his real, as opposed to his assumed name and the way ahead seems clear. Yet it is precisely at this moment that Hugo introduces a dramatic (even melodramatic) *péripétie* – Ruy Blas's suicide – which sets all this at naught. It may be argued that *Ruy Blas* represents an advance on its predecessor in that at least the unity of action is not violated, and Hugo makes do with one dénouement rather than two, but, paradoxically, we might also argue that the avoidance of this duality renders the play's message less clear. Given that Hugo has nailed the colours of his multi-layered interpretation of the play to the mast of his preface, we are entitled to expect him to carry through this interpretation with consistency. The confusion resides in the fact that in *Hernani* the providential figure of the Emperor remains alive, whereas in *Ruy Blas* the providential figure has to die for dramatic purposes. It is increased by the fact that the play begins, symbolically, at dawn: 'Ils dorment encor tous ici. –Le jour va naître' (2). This dawn seems to be that of the accession of the people to power, as Ruy Blas suggests by his words to Don César: 'Tous deux nés dans le peuple, – hélas! c'était l'aurore!' (286), and as he confirms after his Act III interview with the Queen: 'De ma vie, ô mon Dieu, cette heure est la première' (1277). However, the play ends at night, as we see in the stage directions for Act V. Moreover, both Ruy Blas and the Queen, at different times, see happiness epitomised in an untrammelled, open-air existence, yet both finish up in the small, cell-like room in Don Salluste's house. It is as if the world of social fatality has closed in on them in spite of Ruy Blas's achievement in ridding the world of fatality's principal exemplar. [7]

---

[7] There is, of course, the obstacle of history to contend with, in the sense that, whereas Hugo could depict in *Hernani* the triumph of Don Carlos, because Don Carlos did become Emperor, he could hardly show the success of

Notwithstanding this confusion, I think *Ruy Blas* must be seen in terms which, politically, are both consistent with, and an advance on those of *Hernani*. In *Hernani*, the people participate only indirectly: they never appear on stage, but their aspirations are embodied in the sentiments expressed by the reborn Don Carlos. Ruy Blas's attack on the ministers in Act III, scene 2, situated at the very heart of the play, constitutes a direct link with Don Carlos's monologue in *Hernani*: just as Don Carlos had invoked Charlemagne, so Ruy Blas invokes Charles V:

> Charles-Quint, dans ces temps d'opprobre et de terreur,
> Que fais-tu dans ta tombe, ô puissant empereur?
> Oh! lève-toi! viens voir! – les bons font place aux pires.
> Ce royaume effrayant, fait d'un amas d'empires,
> Penche... Il nous faut ton bras! au secours, Charles-Quint!
> Car l'Espagne se meurt, car l'Espagne s'éteint!   (1139-44)

The inference is clear: Don Carlos had appealed to Charlemagne for inspiration, Ruy Blas appeals to Charles V, and himself aspires to be the figure who will re-enact the past glories of the Imperial regime, putting an end to 'L'heure sombre où l'Espagne agonisante pleure!' (1062). Moreover, Ruy Blas's vision of empire is, like that of Charles V, based on the people, and is more genuinely democratic because Ruy Blas himself is of plebeian origin. It is not difficult to see the relevance of such ideas to the state of France in 1838, and it has been suggested that Ruy Blas's tirade embodies Hugo's own dislike of the bourgeois monarchy of Louis-Philippe, and his own aspirations to political status under the patronage of Hélène de Mecklembourg, duchess of Orleans, who perhaps did not find the portrait of the Queen in the play entirely unflattering.[8]

an entirely fictional minister in an ostensibly historical situation. The death of Ruy Blas may, therefore, also be seen in terms of Hugo's situation as a 'prisoner of history'. In all respects other than those I have discussed, the play seems to exemplify Hugo's vision of the social process as enshrined in his essay 'Sur Mirabeau' (1834): see 5, V, 219-21.

[8] A. Ubersfeld argues against this interpretation: 'Penser que Hugo se rêve ami, conseiller, ministre d'une noble souveraine et transpose ce rêve

To underline his political symbolism in the play, Hugo has consistent recourse to the device of disguise. Thus, Don César asks Ruy Blas, when he first appears: 'Cette livrée? est-ce un déguisement?' (279), eliciting the bitter reply: 'Non, je suis déguisé quand je suis autrement' (280). 'Cet habit qui souille et déshonore' (350) symbolises the physical servitude of the oppressed classes to the aristocracy. Apart from this instance, however, disguise does not signify on a physical level in this play, but on a moral level: it is really a *démas-quage*, a means of revealing the true, inner man. Ruy Blas's elevation to the rank of minister, of which he shows himself eminently worthy by his grasp of public affairs, is achieved by way of his disguise as Don César, and in this context, even the name he assumes is important. It implies, of course, that it is in Ruy Blas, the incarnation of the people, that the rightful governing force of nations is to be found, and the entry of God into the equation (1209) indicates that once again, as in *Hernani*, Hugo is putting forward the literal truth of the adage *vox populi, vox Dei*. The Queen underlines the point (although, as she is herself a providential force, the last line of the quotation is in effect tautological):

Va, tu me sembles bien le vrai roi, le vrai maître.
C'est moi, depuis six mois, tu t'en doutes peut-être,
Qui t'ai fait, par degrés, monter jusqu'au sommet.
Où Dieu t'aurait dû mettre, une femme te met. (1245-48)

Ultimately, however, the crown that Ruy Blas possesses is worth more than that of any hereditary monarch:

–O César! un esprit sublime est dans ta tête.
Sois fier, car le génie est ta couronne, à toi! (1274-75)

dans *Ruy Blas*, c'est oublier qu'à la date où il écrit sa pièce, la Duchesse attend l'héritier de la couronne, et que le Duc, bien vivant, n'a rien d'un prince-soliveau' (*4*, I, 16). But this is perhaps to take the examples of the fictional equation rather too literally – one need not assume that Hugo saw himself *exactly* in the situation of a Ruy Blas, as Mme Ubersfeld suggests, but rather more in terms of an *éminence grise*, exercising a beneficial influence on his protectors.

Disguise, then, does not hide, but reveals, in moral terms, the worth of the character. The same interpretation may be applied to the returning Don Salluste, dressed in a valet's livery, the symbolism of which is indicated by Ruy Blas himself: 'J'ai l'habit d'un laquais, et vous en avez l'âme!' (2154). Most interestingly, perhaps, the disguise theme confirms the foregoing analysis of Don César's role in the play. In Act I, he is dressed in 'un bon pourpoint, brodé, passementé' (131) which had previously belonged to the comte d'Albe. By Act IV, this pink satin doublet has become rather the worse for wear, and Don César covers it with a green coat belonging to Don Salluste, and with the latter's name under the collar. Disguise here in each case stresses the links which bind Don César inexorably to the class in which he was born.

It is now time to consider the play in terms of Hugo's theoretical pronouncements on drama, though we should remember that we are now at a remove of more than ten years from the *Préface de Cromwell*, and that, in the intervening period, as successive prefaces had indicated, Hugo had become progressively more concerned with didacticism and less with purely aesthetic questions. There is thus a certain artificiality in discussing the play in terms of the manifesto, although it is not the least of the paradoxes of *Ruy Blas* that in some senses it may be said to conform to the precepts of the *Préface de Cromwell* rather better than *Hernani*.

The unities of time and place are, as we might expect, discarded, although all five acts take place in Madrid, the first three in various parts of the royal palace, the last two in Don Salluste's 'maison discrète' 'à cent pas du palais' (333). The time of the action extends over a period of some six months, the interval essentially elapsing between Acts II and III: the lapse of time is mentioned by the comte de Camporéal (993) and by Ruy Blas himself (1187, 1222). Acts I and II probably take place within a few days of each other: Ruy Blas is described as 'un nouvel écuyer que sa majesté donne / A la reine' (830-1): it is made clear that the marquis de Santa-Cruz has fulfilled his promise to assist the promotion of a man he deems his relative (561, 832); and we learn that Ruy Blas has been absent from Madrid for three days (848). Acts IV and V follow on the day after Act III, the dénouement precipitated by the return of Don Salluste (1480). The unity of action, nowhere to be found in *Hernani*, is clearly present in *Ruy Blas*: although, as we have seen, Hugo confuses the political and dramatic dénouements, he does manage to keep them together. It is arguable that the pace of the play falters slightly in Ruy Blas's address to the ministers (1058-1158), and rather more considerably as a result of Don César's return in Act IV, but there is nothing akin to the enormous dramatic superfluity of Don Carlos's monologue in *Hernani*.

The action, moreover, is much more tightly constructed than had been the case in *Hernani*. There are far fewer implausibilities in motivation and conduct of the intrigue. True, we may well ask how it is that Ruy Blas knows so much about the Queen right from the start, and before he has met her, for example, that 'sa vie est un tissu d'ennuis' (384); and we must also accept that his love for her derives from a typically Romantic *coup de foudre*. Don César, too, knows a good deal more about the Queen's domestic life than would seem likely in one who has been on the road for nine or ten years (413-15); and we wonder, too, how Don Salluste contrives to obtain the lackey's livery disguised in which he enters the palace (1314-16). Hugo has also lost none of his affection for *coups de théâtre* – the mutual recognition of Ruy Blas and the Queen, the return of Don Salluste, and, most clearly, the arrival of Don César via the chimney in Act IV: the fact that, of all the houses in Madrid, he should choose that of Don Salluste, especially when he is unaware of the owner's identity, is really rather hard to accept. Don Salluste's final entry, masked, in Act V, parallels, as we have seen, that of Don Ruy Gomez arrayed in his 'domino noir' in Act V of *Hernani*, but, in contrast, we are spared any repeat of the Gothic mummeries of Act IV of *Hernani*.

Hugo also displays greater consistency in characterisation, and seems at least partially to have resolved the besetting problem of the antithesis between *sublime* and *grotesque*. Don Salluste is consistently *grotesque*, malevolent, egocentric and cruel, and, despite this lack of psychological complexity, remains one of the most successful examples of characterisation

in Hugo's theatre. Notwithstanding his limited number of ap-
pearances, he effectively dominates the action, except for the
brief period in Acts II and III when the idyllic relationship
between Ruy Blas and the Queen moves to the forefront. The
Queen herself evokes his malign and unsettling influence: 'Il
est parti pourtant! je devrais être à l'aise. / Eh bien, non! ce
marquis de Finlas, il me pèse!' (585-6). Don César is similarly
grotesque, but *bouffon* where Don Salluste is *terrible*, and, I
think, similarly though less obviously consistent, for, when
we examine the character closely, we see little evidence of the
sublime. Superficially he is, indeed, a man of honour, as may
be seen in his indignant response to Don Salluste's proposal
in Act I:

> Mais doucement détruire une femme! et creuser
> Sous ses pieds une trappe! et contre elle abuser,
> Qui sait? de son humeur peut-être hasardeuse!
> Prendre ce pauvre oiseau dans quelque glu hideuse!
>
> (239-42)

But his marginality – 'Je suis oiseau, j'aime l'espace' (278)
– and the resultant devil-may-care approach to life lead, as
we have seen, to his being instrumental in the implementation of Don Salluste's scheme, thus rendering him much
more profoundly *grotesque* than at first sight might appear.

The Queen and Ruy Blas are perhaps less successful. The
Queen is, like Doña Sol, *sublime,* but the confusion of political and human levels in her character necessitates, as I have
suggested, an abrupt and not altogether convincing transition
from passivity to dynamism contingent on the arrival of Ruy
Blas. This *sublime* is maintained throughout the play, culminating in her final recognition of Ruy Blas as the 'homme du
peuple' he really is. The eponymous hero, however, is rather
more complex. Certainly Hugo has eschewed the schizo-
phrenic character divisions of *Hernani* – Ruy Blas is *sublime*,
both in love and politics. The grotesque element resides essentially in his social status; in other words it is the mask of
social fatality that prevents him from taking his true position
in society, and which threatens to reassert itself at the end of

the play prior to the Queen's pardon. Hugo's first conception
of the play had placed even greater emphasis on this theme:

> Sa première idée avait été que la pièce commençât par
> le troisième acte: Ruy Blas, premier ministre, duc
> d'Olmedo, tout-puissant, aimé de la reine; un laquais
> entre, donne des ordres à ce tout-puissant, lui fait fermer
> une fenêtre et ramasser son mouchoir.   (5, V, 1398)

The problem with Ruy Blas, as is the case with the Queen,
derives from the confusion of levels. In his relationship with
Don Salluste, Ruy Blas remains essentially passive, apparently subordinating himself to his master's instruction: 'Marchez
les yeux bandés. J'y vois pour vous, mon cher!' (580). The
Queen fires him to action: indeed, if it is true to say, in the
words of a contemporary reviewer, that 'Don Salluste est la
fatalité de la reine, comme Ruy Blas en est la providence',
then it is equally true to say, as we have seen, that the Queen
is the providence of Ruy Blas.[9] For Ruy Blas, however, the
rather unconvincing *psychological* transition from passivity to
energy is paralleled by a similarly unconvincing transition on
the *social* level. Ruy Blas has to adapt from the life and habits
of a lackey to the life and habits of a courtier, an abrupt and
implausible transition which we find it difficult to believe
that he can effect so successfully that no-one suspects anything.

On the formal level, it is clear that Hugo has progressed in
terms of gearing his poetic verve to the content of the play.
The lyricism which constitutes the chief poetic, if not the
chief dramatic beauty of *Hernani* is here kept strictly within
bounds. Indeed the Romantic characteristics of Ruy Blas are
singularly muted; the powerfully rhetorical outbursts of Act I,
scene 3, reminding us of the 'force qui va' side to Hernani's
character, are the more conspicuous because they do not
recur, and there is only one real love duet, in Act III,

---

[9] A. Lireux, 'Détails historiques sur *Ruy Blas*' (*4*, II, 86-90). Mme Ubersfeld argues cogently that Hugo himself is part-author of this article.

scene 3.[10] Even here, we do not find the timeless quality of
the exchanges between Hernani and Doña Sol. For, whereas
the lovers in the earlier play can retreat from the real world
into a world of their own, Ruy Blas and the Queen cannot do
so, because they are involved not only in an emotional, but
in a political relationship: the action of the play admits of
no moments of timelessness into which they can withdraw.
Hernani and Doña Sol forget the world in favour of self-
absorption; Ruy Blas and the Queen must do the precise
opposite:

> Le salut de l'Espagne! – oui, l'Espagne à nos pieds,
> Et l'intérêt public demandent *qu'on s'oublie.*
> Ah! toute nation bénit qui la délie.
> Sauvons ce peuple!   (1352-5; italics mine)

There is, too, I find, a greater naturalism of language in the
love duet, reducing, although not entirely excluding, the level
of stylistic inconsistency that was apparent in *Hernani*:

> Oui, je vais tout lui dire.
> Est-ce un crime? Tant pis! Quand le cœur se déchire,
> Il faut bien laisser voir tout de qu'on y cachait. –
> Tu fuis la reine? Eh bien, la reine te cherchait. (1237-40)

I think this greater naturalism represents an embodiment on
the linguistic level of the greater involvement of the characters in the world and its events. It does not, however, imply
that Hugo has lost any of his skill as a poetic craftsman; as in
Hernani, we see his ability to tailor his verse in order to mirror its content. For example, Ruy Blas's anguished and frenetic jealousy of the King is clearly indicated by the pattern
of stresses in the following lines:

---

[10] It culminates in a kiss, which on the dramatic level parallels the first
(and last) kiss of Hernani and Doña Sol, but which on the political level is
clearly sacramental – Ruy Blas is at the time on his knees before the Queen –
symbolising providential validation of the people's aspirations and efforts.

                    Ecoute.   (2)
Je l'attends tous les jours au passage. Je suis   (3+3+3+3)
Comme un fou. Ho! sa vie est un tissu d'ennuis,   (3+1+2+4+2)
A cette pauvre femme!–Oui, chaque nuit j'y songe.   (4+2+1+3+2)
                    (382-5)

This effect is achieved in a number of ways. Lines 384 and
385 appear 'fragmented', owing to the high number of
stresses. An impression of haste and disorder is created by the
successive *enjambements* of lines 383-4 and 384-5. The
second part of line 384 embodies Ruy Blas's pent-up frustra-
tion and rage in its acerbic assonances of the 'i' (vie, tissu,
ennuis) and the alliteration of the 's' and the 't' (sa, es*t*, tissu).
Line 383 also demonstrates a very subtle 'stuttering' effect
(passage-je), mirroring the near loss of control affecting Ruy
Blas at this time.

   Verbal and poetic virtuosity are similarly much in
evidence. In Act II, scene 5, Hugo contrives to include thirty
répliques in the space of sixteen lines (965-80), whereas Act
IV, in particular, offers the opportunity for *jeux de mots*
('Maison borgne?' 'Non, louche' (1736)), puns ('une duègne,
affreuse compagnonne, / Dont la barbe fleurit et dont le nez
trognonne' (1945-46)),[11] and striking rhymes:

   Lucinda, qui jadis, blonde à l'œil indigo,
   Chez le pape, le soir, dansait le fandango.   (1743-4)

Hugo's handling of history is a curious mixture. To a far
greater extent than *Hernani*, *Ruy Blas* exemplifies the dictum
of the *Préface de Cromwell*: 'l'art...s'étudie à reproduire la
réalité des faits, surtout celle des mœurs et des caractères'.
The poet has in fact taken a good deal of care in his efforts to
achieve authenticity in terms of costumes, decor, and court
ceremonial, as he informs us in his *Note*:

---

   [11] The joke is unfortunately lost on modern readers. Fleury and Trognon
were the authors of history text-books, who taught the children of the King.
Could the joke have been inserted for the benefit of Hugo's patrons, the Duke
and Duchess of Orleans?

> Du reste, et cela va sans dire, il n'y a pas dans *Ruy Blas*
> un détail de vie privée ou publique, d'intérieur, d'ameu-
> blement, de blason, d'étiquette, de biographie, de chiffre,
> ou de topographie, qui ne soit scrupuleusement exact.
> (*3*, p. 197)

However, if this were the main object of the exercise, Hugo
would have produced no more than a well-documented *scène
historique*, and he was well aware that historical documentation must be kept in its place:

> Seulement il croit devoir maintenir rigoureusement
> chaque chose dans sa proportion...Les petits détails
> d'histoire et de vie domestique doivent être scrupuleu-
> sement étudiés et reproduits par le poète, mais unique-
> ment comme des moyens d'accroître la réalité de
> l'ensemble.   (*3*, p. 198)

The attention devoted to the historicity of detail in *Ruy Blas*
leads us essentially to the conclusion that Hugo researched
this *drame* more carefully than any previous play since
Cromwell.[12] And yet it is a curious 'réalité d'ensemble' in
which only one of the four main characters, the Queen, had
any historical existence. Moreover, as our consideration of
the Queen's character might suggest, she is in reality a composite of the two wives of Charles II, Marie-Louise d'Orléans,
gentle, melancholy and oppressed by the ceremonial of the
court, and Anne-Marie de Neubourg, vigorous, dynamic and
forceful, the former offering a historical pattern for the
Queen's conduct in Act II, the latter in Act III. As for
the other characters, all of them are apocryphal. Ruy Blas, the

---

[12] More research has been undertaken on the sources for *Ruy Blas* than
for any other play by Hugo. The poet does not himself specify the titles of the
historical source-works he has used, but critics are generally agreed about his
indebtedness to sets of memoirs by Mme d'Aulnoy, the Marquis de Louville,
and the Marquis de Villars. Most important of all appears to have been the
abbé de Vayrac's *État présent de l'Espagne*. A. Ubersfeld summarises the current state of play on this aspect of Hugo's *drame* (*4*, I, 37-55; II, 71-84). Con-
jectured literary sources are legion, and are again reviewed by Mme Ubersfeld
in her edition of the play (*4*, I, 17-22).

plebeian minister, may have been modelled on Fernando de Valenzuela, the favourite of Marie-Anne of Austria, the queen mother, or on some other *parvenu*, Spanish or otherwise: the fact remains that his ministry is fictitious in its entirety. The family name Bazan Hugo found in his readings of source material, but the forenames Salluste and César are both gallicised versions of Roman (as opposed to Spanish) names, and, since it was not Hugo's habit to gallicise names, we can assume that this is a further pointer to the fact that under the superficially Spanish setting lies a moral more akin to the bourgeois monarchy of Louis-Philippe.

Ruy Blas is something of a curiosity. Hugo clearly attached much significance to its didactic implications, as illustrated not only by his preface, but also in his refusal to tolerate Anténor Joly's class-conscious disposition of seating in the Théâtre de la Renaissance, of which *Ruy Blas* constituted the inaugural production (see *5*, V, 1399-1400). But modern audiences are hardly aware of this level of interpretation, and yet the play continues to be staged. It owes its popularity, I think, to reasons other than those we might advance for the persisting success of *Hernani. Ruy Blas,* once we have accepted the initial implausibility of a lackey in love with a queen, is an extremely well-crafted play, much more coherent than *Hernani*, and written in a verse which, to echo the *Préface de Cromwell*, is "aussi beau que de la prose' (*1*, p. 91). It seems almost unfair that it should not have surpassed *Hernani* in the public's affections, for Hugo's range and mastery of his craft are seen to much greater advantage in *Ruy Blas*. As Fernand Gregh wrote in 1933:

> Tout pesé, c'est peut-être *Ruy Blas* le vrai chef-d'œuvre de Hugo. Certes, *Hernani* a la jeunesse, la jeunesse irrésistible, le sang prompt et étincelant des vingt ans. Mais *Ruy Blas* possède la force complexe de la maturité, ce je ne sais quoi de plus sérieux et de plus profond qui distingue les quarante ans.   (quoted in *3*, p. 223)

5

Epilogue: *Les Burgraves*

WITH an initial run of 49 performances, *Ruy Blas* was a popular, if not a critical, success, and it is therefore all the more surprising that almost five years should have elapsed before the performance of Hugo's next play, *Les Burgraves* (1843). In fact he had begun work in July 1839 on a new play, *Les Jumeaux*, based on the legend of the Man in the Iron Mask, but had stopped writing the following month, having reached Act III, and never resumed work on it. The reasons for this must be conjectural, but it seems quite likely from the fragment we possess that the subject was leading Hugo up the same blind alley he had encountered in both *Hernani* and *Ruy Blas*, in the sense that once again a dichotomy appeared to exist between political and personal salvation: the two young lovers, Alix de Ponthieu and the masked prisoner, are pitted against Cardinal Mazarin, whose entirely laudable political objectives unfortunately cannot permit the prisoner to remain at liberty.[1]

This in turn suggests that Hugo was looking for a dramatic subject, political in orientation, which would allow him effectively to reconcile the two levels, and this he certainly achieved in *Les Burgraves*, ironically the last new play by him to be staged in his lifetime. Contrary to received wisdom, the play should not be seen as a complete failure – it ran for 33 performances – but it was certainly eclipsed by the neo-Classical revival in the shape of Ponsard's *Lucrèce*. Whether this was

---

[1] For reasons which once again involve the theme of the *frères ennemis*, since the eponymous twin brothers are the Man in the Iron Mask and the King, Louis XIV. It should be noted that the play also contains a second, subsidiary, *frères ennemis* theme, the past rivalry of Jean de Créqui and his brother for the love of Alix de Ponthieu's mother (this situation clearly prefigures the Fosco-Ginevra-Donato axis of *Les Burgraves*).

the reason why Hugo wrote no more plays for performance remains, however, an open question.

The preface to *Les Burgraves* abandons the claims for a multi-level interpretation of the play which had complicated the issue with regard to *Ruy Blas*. Hugo insists overtly on the political, indeed on the mythical, dimension of this *drame*. The ostensibly historical subject matter, a conflict set in the Middle Ages between the robber barons of the Rhine and the Holy Roman Emperor, is swallowed up by Hugo's Manichaean vision of the universe which he superimposes on the play. The focus is the centenarian *burgrave* Job and his family:

> Dans une famille pareille, ainsi développée à tous les regards et à tous les esprits, pour que l'enseignement soit entier, deux grandes et mysterieuses puissances doivent intervenir, la fatalité et la providence; la fatalité qui veut punir, la providence qui veut pardonner.
>
> (5, VI, 571)

Fatality is represented by the slave Guanhumara, providence by the Emperor Frederick Barbarossa, and the poet's objective is to achieve a 'grande et morale conclusion' whereby he can 'faire briser la fatalité par la providence, l'esclave par l'empereur, la haine par le pardon' (5, VI, 572).

Job is a somewhat unlikely name for a German baron, but, as in *Ruy Blas*, Hugo's choice aims at symbolic effect rather than verisimilitude. The name symbolises suffering and expiation deriving in this context from two sources, the personal and the political. In the former context, Job, known at the time as Fosco, has (as he believes) killed his foster-brother Donato, and sold the object of their rivalry, the woman Ginevra, into slavery. (Fratricide is, of course, the original and hence archetypal human crime, Abel slain by his brother Cain: see above, p. 60.) In the latter context, he has led the titanic struggle of the Rhineland barons against the authority of the Emperor, but the persistent and unalleviated moral decline of his own family through three generations has convinced him that he has been in error. His country has declined into anarchy, and, on the eve of his hundredth birth-day, Job is left a prey to personal and political remorse.

Job's redemption is first achieved on the political level. A wandering beggar, received at the castle, reveals himself to be none other than the Emperor Frederick Barbarossa, whom all believed drowned on the Third Crusade twenty years pre-viously, but who has returned to save his country. Job's sub-mission to him represents his abjuration of the traditions of his ancestry, the 'Chacun pour soi' mentality of Don Salluste and his ilk; national interest and unity transcend particularist considerations, and Job compels his family to accept the Emperor's suzerainty.

The demise of political fatality is followed by the abol-ition of personal fatality, for which the Emperor is again re-sponsible. This personal fatality is embodied in the slave Guanhumara, the Ginevra of yore, determined to revenge herself on Job-Fosco:

> Je suis le meurtre et je suis la vengeance.
> Je vais, fantôme aveugle, au but marqué d'avance;
> Je suis la soif du sang...
>   ...Je n'ai plus rien d'humain.
> (5, VI, 597; cf. above, p. 61, the juggernaut image)

The implementation of her revenge is prevented by the Emperor, who is revealed also to be Donato, the apparently murdered foster-brother. He pardons Job a second time, and Guanhumara, for no particular reason, it seems, commits sui-cide, thus pointing the message of the play as enshrined in the preface. The Emperor's last speech, prior to his departure, stresses his role as both public and private redemptor:

> J'ai voulu seulement une dernière fois,
> Etendre cette main suprême et tutélaire
> Comme roi sur mon peuple et sur toi comme frère.
>   (5, VI, 648)

So the crime of Cain is symbolically abolished, and the preoccupation with the theme of the *frères ennemis* exor-cised.

Is this perhaps why Hugo stopped writing for the theatre? It is significant that *Les Burgraves* is the only play in which political and personal salvation go hand in hand. It seems unlikely that the less than rapturous critical and audience reception of the play would in itself have been sufficient to deter Hugo from pursuing his career as a dramatist – previous plays had experienced similar resistance. Perhaps, too, he felt that it was time to allow the promise of 1832 to involve himself equally in politics and literature to lapse (see above, p. 58). Certainly the 1840s saw him adopting a more overtly political role, culminating in his nomination as a peer of France. We cannot know for sure.

In spite of recent attempts at critical rehabilitation, Hugo's reputation as a dramatist really does not stand very high today, and I take leave to doubt whether he himself would entirely approve of our contemporary attitudes to these two plays that have stood the test of time. In his preface to *Ruy Blas*, he argues that the theatre-going public divides into three categories: women, thinkers, and 'la foule proprement dite'. And he continues:

> De là, sur notre scène, trois espèces d'œuvres bien distinctes: l'une vulgaire et inférieure, les deux autres illustres et supérieures, mais qui toutes les trois satisfont un besoin: le mélodrame pour la foule; pour les femmes, la tragédie qui analyse la passion; pour les penseurs, la comédie qui peint l'humanité.   (*3*, p. 31)

Hugo believed that the *drame* as he conceived (and executed) it would combine these three elements. But I find it difficult to accept that a modern audience could seriously see in *Hernani* or in *Ruy Blas* either a credible analysis of passion or a plausible depiction of humanity, either in terms of the relationship of man to man, or in terms of a theory of human development. If we enjoy these plays, we enjoy them largely on the level of Hugo's 'foule'. We see in *Hernani* a feeble plot, with whose inconsequentialities we willingly and amusedly collude, somewhat in the way we accept the ludicrous plot-lines of late-night horror films on television. It is a relatively undemanding form of escapism, albeit an escapism with a degree of class, conferred on it by some of the most glorious lyric poetry that Hugo ever wrote. In *Ruy Blas* we find entertainment and enjoyment in the way we might find it in a good detective novel: its structure prefigures that of the 'pièce bien faite' of the later years of the nineteenth century. Once again we delight in the poetry, admiring its virtuosity and fervour, and appreciating the skill of the poet in tailoring it to the content of his play. Nor are the comic scenes of Act IV, if well directed, devoid of the power to amuse.

Such a fate, of course, is not exclusive to Hugo: Voltaire would doubtless turn in his grave to learn that modern readers value *Candide* above *Zaïre* or *Mérope*. But, as we read or watch *Hernani* and *Ruy Blas,* we should also remember that, for Hugo's contemporaries, their significance was altogether different, symbolising the triumph of a cultural reaction against the ossified and stultifying forces of neo-Classicism, and the embodiment of an energetic protest against corrupt, self-seeking and reactionary forms of government. These plays were artistic and political manifestos in action. Even if now, at a distance of a century and a half, they can stand on their own – surely the sign of an enduring work of literature – we should not, for all that, ignore completely what Hugo intended them to be.

Bibliography

i) PRIMARY SOURCES

1. V. Hugo, *Préface de Cromwell*, edited by M. Cambien (Paris, Nouveaux Classiques Larousse, 1972).
2. V. Hugo, *Hernani*, edited by G. Sablayrolles (Paris, Nouveaux Classiques Larousse, 1971).
3. V. Hugo, *Ruy Blas*, edited by G. Sablayrolles (Paris, Nouveaux Classiques Larousse, 1971).
4. V. Hugo, *Ruy Blas*, edited by A. Ubersfeld (Annales littéraires de l'Université de Besançon, vols 121 and 131. Paris, Belles-Lettres, 1971-72).
5. V. Hugo, *Œuvres Complètes*, edited by J. Massin (Paris, Club du Livre, 1967-1970).

ii) SECONDARY SOURCES

6. J.-B. Barrère, *Hugo* (Paris, Hatier, 1967).
   The best general introduction to the poet's life and works. Succinct and helpful assessment of Hugo's output, clearly related to social and political background of 1830s.
7. M. Descotes, *Le Drame romantique et ses grands créateurs* (Paris, Presses Universitaires de France, 1955).
   Very full chronological survey of the stage production of plays in the Romantic period. Includes much detail about the staging of Hugo's *drames*, and places them in the context of other plays being mounted at the time. More useful than the rather gossipy H. Lyonnet, *Les 'Premières' de Victor Hugo* (Paris, Delagrave, 1930).
8. J. Gaudon, *Hugo dramaturge* (Paris, L'Arche, 1955).
   Best general survey of Hugo's theatre in terms of structure, thematic content and critical evaluation. Concise and trenchant, but does not really relate plays' content to the social and political background.
9. T. Gautier, *Histoire du Romantisme* (Paris, Charpentier, 1874).
   Enormously entertaining view of the period by an unashamedly biased eye-witness and participant of the 'bataille d'*Hernani*'.
10. R. B. Grant, *The Perilous Quest* (Durham, N. C., Duke University Press, 1968).
    Extremely stimulating, provocative, somewhat tendentious interpretation of Hugo's literary *œuvre*, containing a chapter (pp. 73-121) devoted to an analysis of the plays of this period. Interesting discussion of the theme of fatality.

11. W. D. Howarth, *Sublime and Grotesque* (London, Harrap, 1975).
Perhaps over-ambitious study of French Romantic drama. Extremely comprehensive coverage militates against depth of analysis, but some critical assessment of each of Hugo's plays of the period.

12. G. Lote, *En préface à 'Hernani'* (Paris, Gamber, 1930).
Useful and interesting survey, especially helpful on the historicity and sources of the play. Perhaps rather over-negative in overall evaluation, lauding the poetry, consigning the rest to oblivion.

13. A. Maurois, *Olympio, ou la vie de Victor Hugo* (Paris, Hachette, [1954]).
Rather disappointingly still the best available biography of the author. Very readable, despite the dated and rather gushing style. Rather too prone to hero-worship. A new hagiography, by H. Juin, *Victor Hugo 1802-1843* (Paris, Flammarion, 1980), is fuller, but covers only the first half of Hugo's life. The somewhat 'breathless', conversational style is a little irritating *à la longue*.

14. A. Ubersfeld, *Le Roi et le Bouffon* (Paris, José Corti, 1974).
The definitive study of Hugo's theatre between 1831 and 1839 (unfortunately excluding *Hernani*). Part I is a meticulously documented history of the writing and production of the plays, and of the (usually hostile) press reaction, together with some interpretative material. Part II, less useful, comprises a rather perplexing analysis of the 'Structures' of Hugo's theatre.